Social Policy and the Young Delinquent

LIBRARY OF SOCIAL POLICY
AND ADMINISTRATION

GENERAL EDITOR: DR. KATHLEEN JONES
Professor of Social Administration
University of York

Social Policy
and the Young Delinquent

by Peter Boss

Lecturer in Social Science
University of Liverpool

LONDON
ROUTLEDGE AND KEGAN PAUL
NEW YORK: HUMANITIES PRESS

First published 1967
by Routledge and Kegan Paul Ltd
Broadway House, 68-74 Carter Lane
London, E.C.4.

Printed in Great Britain
by Willmer Brothers Limited
Birkenhead

© Peter Boss 1967

General editor's introduction

The Library of Social Policy and Administration is designed
to provide short texts suitable for the needs of Social Studies
students in universities and other centres of higher education. They will also be of use to administrators in the social
services, to practising social workers, and to others whose
work brings them into contact with the developing field of
social service.

The Library will provide studies in depth rather than
surveys of the whole field of social policy, and each volume
will be complete in itself. Some will be studies of the British
Social Services. Others will offer accounts of social policy
in other countries, and provide material for comparative
study. A third group will consist of case-studies in the
processes of social policy.

Social Policy and the Young Delinquent is an account of
a process: of the way in which the treatment of the child
delinquent has developed from the days when a boy of
nine could be sentenced to be hanged for stealing two
penny-worth of paint (though, as Mr Boss notes in Chapter
11, the sentence imposed in 1833, was not actually carried

out) to the present controversies concerning the desirability of replacing the legalistic and penal framework of the services for young offenders by a service more appropriate to their educational and social needs.

The publication of the Government White Paper *The Child, the Family and the Young Offender in* 1965 sparked off a controversy of considerable proportions. At the time of writing, the future of the White Paper proposals in England and Wales is still in doubt: and it seems possible that Scottish social policy, based on the Kilbrandon Committee's recommendations of 1964, may develop rather more rapidly in this respect. Scottish experiments may prove a testing-ground for ideas of treatment and rehabilitation still hotly contested in England and Wales.

Mr. Boss deals with the development of policy relating to the young offender with sympathy and clarity. While his own views are progressive, he is at pains to point out the administrative advantages and disadvantages of each of the current proposals, and to leave the reader free to make up his own mind on issues which have no simple and easy solution. Profound changes have taken place in our attitude to delinquent children over the past hundred years, and, as Mr. Boss makes clear, the importance and and even the direction of change was not always clearly discernible at the time. Whatever the outcome of the present controversy, this account of a developing process will be of value in enabling us to stand back and take the long view of one of the most intractable and important problems of modern urban society.

KATHLEEN JONES

Contents

CONTENTS

This book has been written at a time when the government is planning to introduce far-reaching changes in the
policies which apply to the treatment of juvenile delinquents—changes that will have the effect of taking school-
children outside the ambit of juvenile courts and dealing
with them within the educational and welfare services. At
the time of writing, these new proposals have not yet reached
the stage of legislative drafting although they have been
outlined in White Paper form. The matter is still under
discussion. If the proposals do reach the statute book*
a whole chapter will be ended in the history of social
policy in this field, a chapter that has taken almost sixty
years to be written.

What has been done here is to indicate not only present
policy and new ways of thinking, but also what past

*Since this was written there have been press reports that the government
did not intend to proceed with the White Paper proposals, but on 15th
September 1966, Miss Alice Bacon, Minister of State at the Home Office,
addressing the annual conference of the Association of Children's Officers
said: 'Any report that you may have seen that it (the White Paper) is buried
is absolutely untrue'.

policies have been, as it is important that present attitudes should be seen in the context of their historical development. The text itself is intended to be an introductory one only and it is hoped that the interested reader will take his own studies further.

The writer became interested in the subject when, in the course of his occupation as a social worker with a large local authority, he had a good deal of professional contact with the personnel of juvenile courts and knew a great many children who appeared before them. As it was, not only knowing the children, but also knowing their families and their circumstances prompted further enquiry into a subject which has more drama in it and inspires more compassion than can ever be gauged from the bald figures on juvenile crime revealed in the annual criminal statistics or from the reports of chief constables.

It may be of help if something is said about the compass of the book itself and if some of the terms used in it are explained. The situation described is that of England and Wales, but from time to time reference to the Scottish scene is made as well. Practically all the sources to which reference is made are from this country. Material from other countries, notably from the U.S.A., would also have been useful to quote, but it was felt that it would be best to view the British scene, and here Scotland is included, through British eyes. The time span of the developments discussed ranges roughly from the beginning of the nineteenth century to the present time. The term 'policy' has here been taken to mean official policy as adopted by successive governments.

For the most part the age group covered in the discussion about young delinquents is from the present minimum age of criminal responsibility, namely ten years, up to seventeen. It should be pointed out that for present juvenile court procedure, juvenile delinquents are divided up into two age groups: they are 'children' up to the age of fourteen and 'young persons' between the age of fourteen to seventeen years. In the body of the text, to avoid tedious repetition, the terms 'children' or 'juveniles' or 'young delinquents' have been used interchangeably and the division between the legal classification of child and young person has been made only where the context made this necessary. Finally the word 'delinquency'; this can be given a number of different meanings but as written about in this study it means the commission of an act that violates the criminal code and results in a court appearance.

1

Policy influences

It must be said right at the outset that social policy is not always clearly discernible when seen in operation. Much however, can be deduced from current legislation which, so long as it remains extant, may be considered to reflect what the government of the day wishes to be done. Acts of Parliament, statutory regulations and the mass of memoranda of guidance addressed to local authorities, courts of law and other public agencies, all serve to outline the courses of action to be pursued. They are like so many tributaries which run into the main stream of policy. Here we shall be concerned more particularly with policy in relation to juvenile delinquency, the influences which affect its formulation and hence the legislation which gives expression to it. There are the traditional ways of thinking about principles of justice; the duties of the State toward the individual and conversely, the duties of the individual toward the State. There is the prevailing body of knowledge and opinion about the causes and incidence of crime. Of considerable importance, too, is the impact made by the works of individual thinkers, and the comments and suggestions of practitioners in the field of delinquency, such as administrators, psychiatrists, magistrates, social workers and lawyers, making their contributions sometimes as individuals and sometimes jointly through their professional associations. Also important are the various reforming societies which often act as strong pressure groups on those who have the ultimate responsibility for the formulation and implementation of policy.

Social policy is not likely to remain static for long; as new knowledge comes to light, as political power changes in the country and as social and economic conditions alter, so social policies will change also. The pace of change need not be constant but over the space of time, say within the span of a century or so, quite revolutionary changes may occur. So it has been in the case of changes in attitude toward the treatment of juvenile delinquents, amounting practically to a *volte face*, and these have been reflected in social policy. To cite just one example, albeit an extreme one: while it was thought quite an ordinary matter to sentence young children to death by judicial hanging in the 1830s, any proposal for bringing back such a harsh measure, even for a capital crime committed by a child, would nowadays be considered an affront to human decency.

The purpose in this chapter will be to examine some of the influences which have a strong bearing on current thinking about the ways in which young delinquents should be treated, and which have a great deal to do with determining social policy.

Concern over juvenile delinquency

The subject of juvenile delinquency is constantly in the news. Hardly a week passes without a report in the national

6

press of some serious anti-social act which has been committed by a child, whether it happens to be a serious house-
breaking incident or blocking a railway line with rocks in
the path of an oncoming express. Hardly a month passes
without an official pronouncement which expresses anxiety
about the growing prevalence of juvenile crime. Since the
last war, hardly a year has gone by without its statistics of
the increasing numbers of juvenile offenders who have
come before the courts. The incidence of juvenile crime as a
post-war phenomenon is illustrated from comparative
figures produced in the Home Office (1964, p. iiii) Children's Department Report for 1961-1963. These show that for
every hundred children between the ages of eight and fourteen years who were found guilty of indictable offences in
1938, the figure for 1962 had risen to 187, and for the age
group fourteen to seventeen years the numbers in 1962
were as high as 243 in place of each 100 for the pre-war
year. And similar figures, though not of such high proportions, are recorded for the numbers found guilty of non-
indictable offences, or less serious crimes. Even if part of
the increases is accounted for by such factors as greater
police vigilance and more opportunities for committing
offences, the figures still create anxiety and provide a
stimulus for constant reappraisal of measures which may
be applied to reduce them. At the same time it is as well
to view this problem in perspective. Even with the high
figures which, in absolute terms, we have at the present
time, only about 3% of children in the age groups at risk
come before the courts. This fact was recognized in the
Home Office report quoted above when it noted that the
vast majority of boys and girls came through their childhood and youth without ever getting into trouble with the
law.

Having noted that, it is still vitally necessary for the

State to concern itself with this relatively small percentage. It is not something which can be ignored. The whole community is affected by juvenile delinquency and, if not actually harmed, at least irritated by it. As for the juvenile, his delinquency may be a symptom of some deep-seated disturbance which calls for treatment.

Juvenile delinquency is a problem which has exercised the minds of a great many people for a great many years. Social reformers, legislators, criminologists, and individual philanthropists who have thought, written and worked in that field have helped to make a contribution to policy. It is only within comparatively recent times however, that social policy has been designed to aim at *prevention* of delinquency rather than *deterring* the delinquent from committing further offences, through the expansion of the range of the social services.

We shall now discuss some of the influences which are making a contribution to current policy. For the sake of convenience they will be dealt with under separate headings, and it must be taken as axiomatic that these influences overlap and interact with each other; it should not be taken to mean that the order in which they are presented implies that any one of them has to have more importance attached to it than any of the others.

The humanitarian approach

It is currently accepted that children are amongst the more vulnerable groups in our society and therefore require extra protection. As we shall see in the following chapter, this has not always been recognized to the same extent in the past, when they were often considered to be expendable, and, in the process of industrial expansion in the past century, of lesser value than the machines which they

8

tended. Their vulnerability naturally stems from their dependence on adults for their nurture and education. They are subjected to the influences of the world around them and expected to conform to the customs of that world. Thus the child has to learn the system of morals which prevails in his society, more particularly that in his immediate environment, and the knowledge of what is considered to be right and wrong is instilled into him. Since there are frequently doubts about the adequacy of the teaching process, especially that of his parents, and his ability to learn is limited, it has come to be thought unreasonable to expect a child to differentiate clearly between the concepts of right and wrong or to act consistently in a socially approved manner. The younger the child is, the greater will be the consideration extended to him. This is a principle which has in fact been recognized in the criminal law for many hundreds of years; a child of less than seven years of age was deemed incapable of committing a crime since he was not old enough to be expected to know the difference between what was lawful and what was unlawful. The Children and Young Persons Act 1933 raised this lower age limit to eight, and the most recent amendment, in 1963, raised it still further to ten years. So far now, and in the past, does the age of the child form an absolute bar to criminal proceedings. There is an extension of this principle in modified form in respect of children between ten and fourteen years of age. They may be charged with a criminal offence but it is necessary for the prosecution to prove that what was done was known to be wrong by the child and if this cannot be done, then the charge cannot be proceeded with. This legal rule, known as the *doli incapax* rule, has served in the past to mitigate the severity of the law by limiting its application toward children and it remains in existence today. Regard for the child's age in

9

criminal law, is very much in line with other strands of the laws relating to children which merge into the whole pattern of the humanitarian approach. It may, in truth, be said to constitute an expression of the parental obligation which society now collectively assumes towards children generally, and delinquents come in for their share of this attitude. The child in our society is highly placed in the scale of social values and as an American observer (Cohen, 1949, p. 19) put it, 'the way in which children are treated in a society is significant of that society's values.'

The child, because of his age, is protected more against the harsh facts of life than the adult, and this protection is extended to him even when, having broken the law, he comes before the court.

The self-interest of society

From what has been said in the foregoing section it might be assumed that society's motives for the treatment of young delinquents stem from altruism alone. This is not necessarily so. Other motives come into play and writers have stressed the functional value of a differential approach toward children as compared with adults. This is illustrated by the motive of societal self-interest.

It is fortunate that the majority of crimes which are committed by children are not of such a nature that they constitute a serious menace to the safety and welfare of society, even though the prevalence of, say, gang delinquency can look threatening. But the very serious offences in the criminal calendar, such as murder, robbery with violence or rape, about which society could justifiably need to protect itself, feature comparatively rarely in the juvenile crime statistics. By far the largest proportion of indictable offences committed by the young, about nine-tenths of crimes, are either of the breaking-and-entering or larceny types. These, while not to be regarded as trivial matters which one can overlook, can be said to have nuisance value rather than form a serious threat to the social order. The recognition of this led Margery Fry to comment: 'Though a child can do heavy damage, can commit serious crime, the motive of fear, the desire for self-protection on the part of the community, is in his case, largely absent. Or rather it is fear deferred. The young delinquent menaces society by the likelihood of his becoming later an adult criminal, perhaps an habitual one' (see Fry *et al.*, 1947, p. 17). Although Walker (1965, p. 314) has pointed out that positive correlation between an early childhood start and a criminal career later in life has not yet been produced, there is a wide belief that the chances of reclaiming a delinquent are greater when he is young than when he is older and, as Fry pointed out: 'in the case of the child or adolescent the community can, without grave risk, set itself the task of reclaiming a potential enemy at an age when success is most likely.' In this way an enlightened self-interest reinforces humanitarian precepts. Time and trouble spent on the young can save society expense and recrimination later on. Therefore the differential treatment of the young delinquent becomes prudent policy.

The contributions of criminology and the part played by official enquiries

Toward the end of the nineteenth century the relatively new sciences of psychology, anthropology and sociology began to arouse interest, and were influential in providing new insights into the nature of man and his society. They played their part too in focusing attention on the nature of the delinquent, who came to be seen not as a sinful

11

being who stood in need of moral redemption, but more as a victim of circumstances over which he could have little if any control. These new fields of study in turn provided the basis for another newcomer to the social sciences, namely criminology, which has been defined as the science that studies the social phenomenon of crime, its causes, and the measures which society directs against it' (Jones, 1962, p. 1).

Causal explanations of crime have ranged over many theories in their time. Some have concerned themselves with the physical characteristics of the individual. Others have concentrated on specific types of temperament, the incidence of intellectual sub-normality among delinquents, and criminality in terms of the individual's abnormal behaviour. Other theories still abandoned the 'individual' approach and concentrated study on social factors, advancing the proposition that crime is a product of the forces at work in society, for example poverty or unemployment. Family make-up provided another field for enquiry and the frequent number of instances in which delinquents were found to come from broken families gave rise to the theory that the 'broken home' is an important factor in criminality. In recent years criminological research has derived from investigations in what are described as 'delinquency areas', where activities which society at large would term as delinquent, are considered to be normal, socially sanctioned activities in a locality. The advances made in the study of sociology, have also produced important criminological theories, suggesting that criminal behaviour, like other forms of behaviour, is learned by the individual from his environment. The subject of family relationships has provided another field for enquiry in the past few years. Many delinquents have been found to be emotionally disturbed, and this has been traced to a type of family background in which lack of parental affection and unusually high inter-personal stress tend to feature.

While some of these theories treat the problem of criminality in terms of the individual's physical or psychological constitution, others treat it in terms of social factors, either in connection with his immediate environment or with the wider society of which he is a member. 'Not one of the criminological theories', says Howard Jones (1962, p. 103), 'provides a satisfactory explanation of all criminal behaviour. Each throws some light on the problem, perhaps explaining some certain kinds of criminal behaviour, or certain of the facts empirically found associated with delinquency.' The complexities involved in making any kind of investigation into the causes of delinquency for the purpose of testing theory are many. At the same time, there is little doubt that the weight of research findings has profoundly affected the thinking of those directly associated with problems of delinquency. Much of the research relating to crime generally has been undertaken in relation to juvenile delinquency, so that the research data have been drawn directly from that field in many cases.

Because research has suggested that the young delinquent is subject to interacting psychological and sociological forces, this view has been reflected in modern treatment measures.

It has become established practice for governments to keep themselves informed about matters which affect social policy through appointing commissions or committees of enquiry from time to time. This could be termed another form of research, although it lacks the more rigorous, scientifically devised methods of the academically orientated investigations. But the objective is similar. Commissions or committees are set terms of reference for the field with which their enquiry is to be concerned and they then proceed to gather together and sift available relevant opinion and information. The process usually includes hearing of evidence from corporate bodies and individuals. The reports which finally result from this contain recommendations which the government may subsequently translate into policy through legislation. In the field of juvenile delinquency there have been many such inquiries since the commencement of the nineteenth century. Each one makes interesting reading about prevailing knowledge and opinions and enables us to see the background to policies and changes in policies so making the picture more intelligible. And of course, these official enquiries provide their share of the influences under discussion.

Consideration for the young delinquent's educational and social needs

The last mentioned point brings us to a brief consideration of the recent suggestion for a radical change in policy. Powerful arguments are being put forward to suggest that the young delinquent should be dealt with within the framework of the ordinary education system, with the aid of support for himself and his family by such social services as are provided by local authority children's departments and parts of the health, and welfare services. The needs of the handicapped pupil in school are already recognized, and categories of handicaps for educational purposes have been established for which special educational facilities can be made available. Educationally sub-normal children and maladjusted children are two such groups. They may receive special attention to their needs, sometimes in the ordinary school, sometimes in a special school. Modern educational policy favours the former method. It may be claimed that the delinquent child presents another form of

14

handicap and setting him apart from other children serves no particularly useful purpose. To this may be added, that many children who commit acts which would undoubtedly render them liable to criminal proceedings, are dealt with in other ways by teachers and others who have authority over them. It may be advanced that the dividing line between those considered as maladjusted by the education service and those who appear before court as delinquent is often not a clear one. Many children find their way into schools for the maladjusted only after their appearance before court, and in some cases the court appearance has been used as a means of getting them to such a school. The Children's Departments often receive into their care those who have committed offences but who have not been prosecuted; and treat them in the same manner as children who have not demonstrably broken the law. The same 'accidental' nature of the course of action can be applied in these cases. It is often a matter of chance whether a child is brought before a court or dealt with from the outset by the education or social services.

These ideas which have been canvassed for a relatively short period have brought a powerful stimulus to thinking and proposals for a change of policy.

The blurring of the distinction between delinquent and non-delinquent children

One of the most interesting and far reaching effects of social policy in recent times has been the erosion of the sharp distinction between those children who come before the juvenile courts because they have committed offences and those who require care, protection or control. In the case of this latter group, the State intervenes because it is considered that these children require some form of pub-

lic protection on account of their age and circumstances
It may be that offences, such as physical assault, have been
committed against them, or that they have been neglected
by their parents, or that they have got into moral danger
or are said to be beyond parental control. Truants from
school too come into this category. The process of defining
the care, protection or control category of children
commenced in the last century, the first major enactment
being the Prevention of Cruelty and Protection of Children
Act 1889. Since that date various amending acts have
enlarged the definition of circumstances as a result of which
children may be brought before the court for protective
purposes. The most recent legislation in the series is in the
Children and Young Persons Act 1963, under which it has
been made possible for the court to deal with a child under
the age of ten years on a protective, and therefore, non-
criminal basis in such circumstances which, previously
would have rendered him liable to criminal proceedings.
Before 1963, an eight-or nine-year-old who had committed
larceny could be brought before the juvenile court as an
offender and his case would eventually feature as a relevant
statistic in the annual returns of juvenile crime. Today he
may still be brought before the court, not as a juvenile
delinquent, but on the grounds that the court should intervene because he is not receiving the care, protection and
guidance which a good parent might reasonably be expected to give him.

Not infrequently the grounds for dealing with one child
on a criminal, and with another, on a non-criminal basis,
stem from the same set of circumstances. For instance,
the boy who indecently assaults a girl may come before
court as a juvenile delinquent. The girl may also appear
at the same court, but as requiring care, protection or
control, or, in other words, as a non-delinquent. The treat-

16

ment facilities which the courts have at their disposal may in some cases be identically applied to both cases. Both these children could be removed from home and placed in separate approved schools, but they could also be committed to the care of the local authority, and this could well be the same local authority for both of them.

The dividing line between the two categories is frequently a very indistinct one. This point was made as far back as 1924 in a Home Office Children's Department Report (p.11) in which it was remarked that: 'the commission of an offence is usually incidental to neglect on the part of the parents, and it may be merely chance that one child is charged with an offence and another is found wandering'; and much the same comment was reiterated in another official document, the Report of the Care of Children Committee (Curtis Committee, 1945-46, para. 38). Since then the point has not escaped the notice of students of juvenile delinquency (Kahan, 1961 who makes the point that 'non-offenders are often only accidentally' not delinquent). This line of thought has led to the further extension of the range of non-criminal procedures, and has led to the current suggestion of a total departure from judicial procedures in such cases.

Conclusion

The influences which have a strong bearing on the formulation and execution of social policy are many and various. They may come quickly or linger and remain dormant for many years. At the present time, having experienced a period of relative quiescence for the best part of sixty years during which there have been no radical departures from established procedures, since, in effect, the introduction of the juvenile court system through the Children Act in 1908, we are likely to be entering a period of important changes for the juvenile delinquent and society at large.

Opinion about the right and wrong way of dealing with juvenile delinquents can show considerable variations, but in broadly defined terms, society has now committed itself to a liberal and humanitarian policy in the expectation that such a policy is likely to pay dividends in the future. Much of this is based on faith in that it is not possible to state at present what sort of policy, liberal or harsh, yields better results. Since it is known, however, that much of juvenile delinquency occurs in the socially, educationally and economically underprivileged groups, social justice alone demands that this is taken into account in devising policy. Where, otherwise, delinquency is due primarily to psychological maladjustment, policies must take account of this factor also and be practically expressed in such a way that they heal rather than punish.

We are moving further and further away from the concept that the young delinquent is someone against whom society must be protected. In its place we are nearer the stage where he is likely to be dealt with outside the ambit of the criminal law altogether and treated like any child who requires guidance and protection such as can be provided by the existing educational and social services.

2
The historical background —
from retribution to reform

Common law in relation to the young delinquent in the early years of the nineteenth century

When one considers the humanitarian and liberal attitude which society today adopts toward the young delinquent, it is salutary to remember that it has taken a considerable time to achieve this reversal of policy. The treatment of the young delinquent, both in the legal procedure associated with his trial, as well as in the ways he is dealt with after trial by the court, bears a very different stamp now from that of a century and a half ago. At that time, policy was influenced considerably by the prevailing moral view that crime was not only an offence against society but also an offence against God, a sin, which had to be purged. Harsh punishment of the young was meant for their ultimate salvation and not something that should be shirked. The principles of common law governed policy and determined the manner in which old and young alike were treated.

Of these principles there was the important one of equality before the law. If a child was charged with an indictable offence, that is to say, one which was triable by a jury, he was liable to appear before a higher court than the petty sessional court, in which all the pomp and majesty of the law was displayed and strict formality of procedure observed. Furthermore, as a logical extension of the principle of equality, if convicted of the offence he became subject to the same punishments as an adult, and punishment was graded either by statute or judicial precedent. Where courts dealt more leniently with children on account of their age, as often was the case, it must be supposed that this was due to the discretionary element in sentencing allowed to the court rather than to something specifically granted in law or encouraged by it in the case of children. The effect of this was that children might expect to be treated compassionately, but could not receive any differential treatment from the law as of right.

The punishment of children

Certainly at the commencement of the nineteenth century it was by no means considered unreasonable that children should be sentenced to death, transportation or imprisonment. According to Colquhoun (see Hinde, 1951, p. 42), who was writing at the turn of the century, the number of capital offences for which hanging was prescribed as the penalty exceeded one hundred and sixty. Transportation to the colonies was the common experience of the habitual offender, and imprisonment the lot of those whose misdeeds were not serious enough to warrant the application of sterner measures.

As late as 1833 a boy of nine was sentenced to be hanged for the comparatively trivial offence of poking a stick through a patched up pane of glass and stealing two pennyworth of paint, although it is only fair to record that the

20

sentence was not carried out (see Du Cane, 1885, p. 18). As for transportation, while young children might escape that punishment on account of their tender age, it was stated in evidence to the House of Lords Committee on Juvenile Delinquency and Transportation 1847, that 339 boys between the ages of fourteen and seventeen years were transported in 1844 alone. But normally the punishment for juveniles was likely to be imprisonment. The Recorder of Dublin, the Right Honourable F. Shaw, told the same committee that in the case of children he generally gave three months for a first and ordinary offence, six months for a second one, and for a third, if it was a young boy, twelve months instead of transportation.

In 1816, Du Cane recorded that when the population of London was somewhat less than two and a half million, the prisons in the town held about 3,000 inmates under the age of twenty years—half of these being under seventeen, and some as young as nine or ten (see Du Cane, 1885, p. 200). In 1835, 6,803 young people, one in 449 of the population between ten and twenty years, were in prison; in 1844 there were 11,348 or one in 304 of the total population in that age group, and in 1853 nearly 12,000 children and young persons were sent to prison in that one year alone. Apparently imprisonment was the only way the State would or could think of dealing with the rising numbers of delinquents produced perhaps by the *laissez faire* nature of industrial expansion and the rapid growth of towns. Little attempt was made to do anything positive and constructive once the young offender was in prison. Those few ameliorating measures that were introduced by the State during the first half of the century were restricted in objective.

Misgivings as to the usefulness and morality of sending children to prison had been voiced in an early official report, that of the Committee on Prisons and Penitentiaries (1811) which considered it 'highly inadvisable that young persons of twelve or thirteen should be exposed to the instruction of those who can initiate them in all the mysteries of fraud and villainy'; but Parliament took no action on this critical comment. The State's concern was with punishment, and if the young committed crimes then they, in the same way as the adults, had to receive their just deserts. This attitude was deeply entrenched and as one writer has pointed out, it took Parliament the first fifty years of the nineteenth century to change it and to commence the adoption of a policy which was directed toward reform rather than merely punishment (Hinde, 1951, p. 95).

Early reformatory measures

The eighteenth century had already thrown up a number of voluntary ventures which were devoted to the care and upbringing of children whose conditions were such that they might easily fall into crime. Of such, the Marine Society established in 1756, was, in the words of one of its staunchest supporters, Jonas Hanway, given over to the reception of boys 'whose daring tempers . . . may subject them to become victims of the law'. The Philanthropic Society, was founded in 1788 to provide care and upbringing for children whose parents were convicted felons and who had been left bereft of a home through their parents subsequent death or exile; and in addition for juvenile delinquents themselves. Other voluntary organizations such as the Prison Discipline Society 1815, and a farm colony at Stretton-on-Dunsmore in Warwickshire established by local philanthropists around 1817, followed on the principles established by the earlier organizations. Some courts encouraged the work of these various bodies by granting

22

pardons to young offenders instead of ordering imprisonment, on condition that they placed themselves under the care of one of these charitable institutions. This depended on the offenders' voluntary co-operation, for the managers of the institutions had no legal power of detention.

As for the State's own efforts, a modest beginning upon reform was made when, in 1838, Parliament passed the Parkhurst Act. This provided for the exclusive use of Parkhurst prison for juveniles between the ages of ten and eighteen years who had been sentenced to transportation. Instead of being sent overseas they were to remain at the prison for two or three years for the purposes of training and after that time were subject to compulsory emigration. In point of fact they were usually released after having served their time in prison. The preamble to the Act is worth a mention here as it expresses so well the prevailing attitude of those years:

It is a great public Advantage that a Prison be provided in which young Offenders may be detained and corrected and receive such Instruction and be subject to such Discipline as shall appear most conducive to their Reformation and to the Repression of Crime . . .

The emphasis was obviously more on discipline than anything else and the regime was so harsh that, as Mary Carpenter commented (on p. 321) in her book *Reformatory Schools* in 1851, 'it attempted to fashion children into machines through iron discipline instead of self-acting beings.' Following its inception in 1838, the prison received fewer and fewer children as the years went by, so that while in 1849 there were 700, and in 1854, 536, the numbers had dwindled to 68 by 1884, the year in which the establishment closed down.

While the Parkhurst system in practice came to be little more than a juvenile prison, in principle it had been conceived of as providing reformatory treatment. It serves as an early example of an attempt to differentiate treatment between adult and child and also began the process, which led away from use of punishment alone, toward reform of the young delinquent through education, vocational training, and humanitarian interest and concern.

The reformatory movement was beginning to get under way in earnest toward the middle of the century, although the actual number of institutions, supported at this time from private, charitable sources, was not great—hardly more than thirty in number. The Home Office had already shown some interest in their use, offering money towards the running costs of at least one in 1843, but Parliament at that time was not yet persuaded of their value. Efforts however continued to be made to convert the legislature to the idea that reformation of young delinquents in these schools offered more hope of success than could the prisons with their downright repressive facilities. The evidence which had been given to the House of Lords Committee had done a good deal to publicize the evils which the imprisonment of children produced. In addition there were the revelations of Mary Carpenter, that indefatigable worker on behalf of the reformatory schools, who quoted extensively from the report in her book in which she pleaded with powerful logic and persuasion for, what she called, the children of the 'perishing and dangerous' classes. The former she described as, 'those who had not yet fallen into actual crime but who were almost certain from their ignorance, destitution and the circumstances in which they were growing up, to do so, if a helping hand be not extended to raise them,' and the latter—the 'dangerous'

24

classes, those 'who had already received the prison brand, or if the mark had not yet been visibly set upon them, were notoriously living by plunder—who unblushingly acknowledged that they could gain more for the support of themselves and their parents by stealing than by working.'

Her analysis of the incidence as well as the effects of juvenile delinquency, her round condemnation of the prison system as a viable means of reform for young delinquents, and her urgent plea for the State to interest itself in the use of such schools, industrial schools for the children of the 'perishing classes' and reformatory schools for those of the 'dangerous classes', made an important contribution to the eventual adoption of these very measures by the State not many years later.

Her efforts and those of others like her were reinforced by the mounting interest in the need for a state-provided system of elementary education for children of all classes. Althought the first great Education Act did not come into operation until 1870, those voluntary societies which were providing education for the masses, albeit in sketchy fashion, were already receiving some financial support from the State. The principle of government support in this field had become established before the middle of the century, and it might not have been too much to hope that it would similarly become established in the case of industrial and reformatory schools, in which particular emphasis was laid on the value of educational programmes.

In 1853, largely as a result of a conference on the need for reformatory schools for young delinquents, convened by Mary Carpenter and Matthew Davenport Hill, Recorder of Birmingham, a House of Commons Committee was set up to consider, yet once more, the treatment of juveniles who had broken the law. This time the committee came

25

out strongly in favour of a new system of teatment which would make use of the industrial and reformatory schools, support them financially out of public funds and bring them under government inspection. Previously Parliament had not been ready to take any action because, as Cohen (1949, p. 31) remarks, 'it was said that the mind of the public was unprepared for change', but now it was prepared to do so. Even so, the provisions that were made were scarcely imaginative or generous.

The reformatory and industrial schools Acts

The first Act was passed in 1854 and related to Scotland only; under it, vagrant, mendicant or homeless children under fourteen years of age could be sent by a court to any reformatory or industrial school in that country. A little later in that same year, the Reformatory School (Youthful Offenders) Act made similar provisions for England and Wales. By it, young offenders under the age of sixteen years could be sent to one of the reformatory schools and detained there for from two to five years, but only *after* they had served a sentence of imprisonment of not less than fourteen days. Reformatory schools were not to be used as an alternative to prison but rather as a supplement to it. Lord Russell, when introducing the Bill, had expressed the hope that Parliament, by adopting the system, 'might be able to effect to some measure that the young offenders sent to these institutions would forget their vicious habits in them and be restored as respectable and useful members of society' (Hansard, H. L., 1854). But those 'vicious habits' had first to be tamed in prison, for Parliament, with the exception of only a few members, seemed convinced that it was dealing here with morally culpable children. Punishment by imprisonment, as a precedent for reformatory school treatment, continued right up to 1899, when it was finally abolished.

To meet the criticism of those who thought that families might well encourage their children to commit crimes so that they might be rid of their maintenance during the prolonged sojourn at the schools, parents were required to contribute toward the cost according to their means. Another reason for incorporating this provision into the legislation stemmed from the belief that parents should be made to feel responsible for the conduct of their children. Throughout all the numerous amending and initiating legislation that followed the Acts of 1854, this contributory principle remained official policy and still remains so at the present day. It could never be claimed, nor can it now, that parental contributions have made any significant difference to costs. In 1859 their share was little more than 2% of the total costs from public funds which them amounted to some £73,000 and in 1882, when the State paid out £134,000, parents contributed rather less than 5% of that sum.

Following on soon after the Acts of 1854, a series of legislation confirmed that the State had come to accept the concept of reforming young delinquents through training and education in the schools. In 1857, two Acts, for reformatory and industrial schools respectively, made it possible for public funds to be expended in building new schools or extending existing ones, and further legislation in 1866 consolidated what had been achieved up to then.

At last the State began to accept its responsibility for greater differential treatment of young offenders, and thought in terms of reform rather more than punishment.

The initial distinction between reformatory and industrial schools became lost as time went by. In 1896, the Departmental Commitee on Reformatory and Industrial

Schools reported that the only remaining difference lay in the ages of the children. In practice those up to sixteen years of age were generally found to be in the industrial schools, whilst the older ones, between sixteen and twenty-one, were in the reformatory schools; but the titles of the schools remained distinct right up to 1933, when through the Children and Young Persons Act they were both restyled 'approved schools', approved that is to say, by the Secretary of State, 'for the education and training of children committed to them by the courts.'

Other measures of reform

Social policy in respect of reforms in the treatment of young delinquents was not exclusively concerned with the reformatory and industrial schools movement. Important as this movement was in marking changes in policy, there were others which, while not immediately attracting much publicity, provided their share in the sum total of important reformatory measures which culminated later in the great Children Act of 1908.

One of these reforms lay in the modification of trial procedures as applied to children. The application of the principle of equality before the law resulted in equal treatment of all who came before the courts irrespective of age. It was common enough for an eight-year-old child to have to stand trial at quarter sessions or assizes if he had committed an indictable offence. One way in which the impact of such procedure could have been lessened would have been for courts at the lower level to deal with children's indictable offences on a summary basis, thus avoiding the necessity for trial by jury at a higher court. A Royal Commission which had been set up in 1836 to consider whether any distinction should be made in the mode of trial between adult and juvenile offenders had been unable to recommend such a course of action and it was left to the Select Committee of the House of Lords on Juvenile Offenders and Transportation, 1847, to press for increased use of summary jurisdiction in the case of children. This recommendation was accepted by Parliament and in that year magistrates were given power to try children under the age of fourteen on a summary basis for simple larceny. It should be noted, that this was a power, not a duty. Its exercise lay within the discretion of the magistrates to be applied by them in any particular case. This power was later extended in the Summary Jurisdiction Act 1879, by which children under twelve years of age could be dealt with summarily for all indictable offences, and young persons between twelve and sixteen could also receive summary trial in the case of such indictable offences as larceny and embezzlement. The immediate benefits which accrued to young delinquents as a result of these reforms were that they no longer had to undergo trial by jury, and that summary jurisdiction usually involved milder sentences.

The power of magistrates to apply summary jurisdiction did not become a general duty until the implementation of the Children Act 1908, after which only homicide and offences committed in certain defined circumstances involved initial proceedings in courts other than the specially created juvenile courts.

Another indication of the gradually changing policy towards juvenile delinquents comes from the use of guardianship proceedings. In 1840 the Infant Felons Act made it possible for the Court of Chancery to assign the care and custody of a person under the age of twenty-one years who had been committed for felony to anyone willing to take charge of him; but here too, (as was the case later when children could be sent to the reformatory schools) only after a term of imprisonment was served first. Even such a seemingly moderate measure met with vigorous opposition in Parliament, as constituting interference with the rights of parents to the custody of their children. The provision was little used, but it serves as yet one more signpost along the road of reform.

The probation system now so widely used as a suitable treatment measure, provides yet another example of changing attitudes. Its early origins derived from the discretion in sentencing employed by some of the magistrates in Warwickshire in the 1820s, who, instead of committing a child to prison, might grant him a pardon on condition that he returned to the care of his parent or master to be more carefully supervised by him in the future. This practice was later adopted by Matthew Davenport Hill in the 1840s when he had become recorder for Birmingham and featured in a report to Parliament in 1847 (Hansard, H. C., 1847) when an attempt was made to win over the House of Commons and gain legislative backing. But Parliament was at that time unwilling to give its blessing to such a novel proposal. Once again, it required voluntary effort to provide the much needed impetus. This came in 1876, when the Church of England Temperance Society, anxious to expand its social work, appointed a missionary worker to visit some of the Metropolitan police courts and attempt the reclamation of drunkards. Drunkenness featured to a considerable extent amongst offences committed by children as well as adults. For example in Liverpool, in 1877, arrests for 'being drunk and disorderly' included 97 boys and 18 girls under the age of ten years and 217 boys and 32 girls between the ages of ten and twelve. So much in demand was the society's work in the police court mission field, that by 1900 there were some 119 missionary workers serving the various magistrates' courts (King, 1964, p. 3).

The State eventually endorsed the principle of probation, although it was not until 1887 that the initial Probation of First Offenders Act was passed and even then provision for statutory supervision was left out; this had to await further action under the Probation of Offenders Act 1907.

Interest in juvenile delinquency declined as the nineteenth century drew to a close. It may have been thought at that time that the advances already made were sufficient not only in making treatment more humane but also in bringing about a reduction in the volume of delinquency. Instead interest shifted to those categories of children who were being cruelly treated and neglected by their parents. The National Society for the Prevention of Cruelty to Children had been formed out of a number of separate societies which had been operating in London, Liverpool and other large provincial cities. Supported by the patronage of influential philanthropists and politicians, it worked hard to draw attention to the plight of large numbers of children who suffered cruelty or neglect under the care of their parents. The parents' right to custody could not be touched by the existing law mainly out of consideration for the principle of the inviolability of the family; for what a parent did to and with his children was very largely his own affair and no business of the State. The society, however, was able to demonstrate the extent to which children were exposed to suffering, and brought about the strengthening of the law with a number of statutory provisions. The first of these was the Prevention of Cruelty and Protection of Children Act 1889, which enabled the courts to intervene on behalf of these children, and where necessary take steps to remove them from their unsuitable environment. The first Act, one commentator has said, possessed powers of protection that were new in English social history and expressed the public desire to try and prevent cruelty to any child before it actually occurred (Heywood, 1959, p. 102).

The juvenile courts

Although the introduction of the juvenile court system in this country was a product of the twentieth century, it justifies its place in this chapter because it seems to round off the achievements of the nineteenth. Relaxation of trial procedures, differential treatment of delinquents after finding of guilt in the court and a generally less rigid attitude toward juveniles' misbehaviour brought about through better understanding of the social problems which give rise to it, produced a new climate of opinion likely to favour the next important advance in social policy. Toward the end of the nineteenth century, some magistrates in Birmingham had commenced the practice of dealing with the cases of young delinquents at times that were distinct from other court sittings in order that they might not have to associate with adult offenders who were awaiting their turn at trial. In the Children Act 1908, this practice was legalised through the provision of the juvenile courts. These were to be magistrates' courts possessing summary jurisdiction, empowered to deal with all juveniles under the age of sixteen years convened either at a different time or in a different place from other court sittings. There was more involved than just the separation of the young from older offenders. Restrictions were placed on persons who could attend court, the general public being excluded, and parents could be required to attend with their children; thus once again the principle of parental responsibility for their conduct was underlined. Imprisonment for children under sixteen was abolished except in certain defined cases,

32

delinquent children could be committed to the care of fit persons, and remand in custody was in future to be undergone in specially provided homes instead of in prisons. (It should be noted that while the Children Act 1908 brought in the juvenile court system, it was also an important amending and consolidating measure gathering together much of the law relating to children which had accumulated over the preceding fifty years or so.)

The concept of the juvenile court was something new in this country. It was aimed at the treatment of juvenile delinquents as well as those who required the State's protection on account of parental cruelty or neglect. As a result the magistrates' courts came to exercise sometimes a criminal jurisdiction and sometimes a protective, or Chancery Court type of jurisdiction, depending on whether they were dealing with a child who had broken the law, or one who was considered to be in need of 'care or protection'. This policy was not entirely new as the magistrates had been used to applying these procedures since the children's protective legislation of 1889, but now both could be seen operating in the one type of court.

The juvenile court system has withstood the test of time up to the present. Since its inception, two governmental committees of enquiry, the Committee on the Treatment of Young Offenders, 1927, and the Committee on Children and Young Persons, 1960, have reaffirmed their faith in it as the proper agency to deal with juvenile delinquents. The only major inter-war legislation for juvenile delinquency, the Children and Young Persons Act 1933, made no changes of any importance in its constitution and competence and as one historian of penal policy has commented, 'it is a remarkable tribute to the soundness of the principles upon which the 1908 Act was built when it is realized that a quarter of a century later no revolutionary change was found to be necessary' (Hinde, 1951, p. 173). It is only in comparatively recent times that the whole support on which the principles for dealing with young delinquents has been based has come in for rethinking, but we shall leave consideration of that matter until Chapter 5.

Conclusion

The nineteenth century was prolific in legislation which was directly aimed to benefit children. Sir William Clarke Hall noted that during the reign of Queen Victoria more than a hundred such Acts were passed (Heywood, 1959, p. 150). But many of these got on the statute book only after considerable opposition by Parliament and society at large. This need not surprise us because many of the suggested changes threatened to upset firmly held doctrines which stemmed from a strict moral code that equated crime with sin. To give ground therefore, must have seemed to many quite sincere people as constituting a denial of fundamental and cherished beliefs. And concessions once granted, who could say what the next round of proposals would not produce, all in the name of reform? But the social order itself was changing. The second half of the nineteenth century was less stark in economic and social terms than the first half had been and reform was generally in the air, not only in the manner of treatment of juvenile delinquents. Thus the strictly punitive attitude which was so common a feature at the commencement of the century gradually abated. The use of prisons for the young offender gradually yielded to the use of reformatory and industrial schools; the number of juveniles under the age of sixteen who were committed to prison dropped from 16,000 about the middle of the century to less than 1,700 by its close.

34

In 1857 the reformatory schools housed 2,300 boys and girls. By the end of the period they had charge of some 30,000, while an additional 3,000 attended industrial day schools (Grünhut 1948, p. 373).

Gradually too, the principle of equality before the law was encroached upon in respect of trial proceedings, and juveniles were being treated with greater discrimination. In fact young people emerged as a distinct group to whom more liberal measures were applied than to adults, and much of what was being done for them became the pattern for policies for adults later.

The Children Act 1908 crystallized into social policy attitudes which had been changing for the best part of the preceding century, and the Act stands out today as a paramount landmark in the history of the treatment of delinquency.

3

Juveniles before the court

The jurisdiction of the juvenile court

Whatever the pattern for dealing with young delinquents might be in the future, at present it is based on the juvenile court system. For that reason this chapter will be concerned with a description of its jurisdiction, procedure and competence.

English juvenile courts are courts of criminal jurisdiction with an additional competence in non-criminal matters (see Grünhut, 1948, p. 354). It is the trial of offences which constitutes the major part of the business of these courts, and the ordinary laws of the land are administered, although there are modifications of procedure. However, Cavenagh (1959, p. 60) has pointed out that 'it is in the methods available to the juvenile courts *after* the charge has been proved that most scope has been given for differentiating between adults and juveniles'. So far as the actual trial is concerned, a child is not denied rights that also belong to an adult, and this principle of jurisdiction had been the cause of confirmatory comment in official reports since it first became fixed as part of the juvenile court law in the Children Act 1908. The Committee on the Treatment of Young Offenders, the Moloney Committee of 1927 (p. 19), advanced two reasons for supporting the criminal jurisdiction of the juvenile court:

1. In the first instance it is very important that a young person should have the fullest opportunity of meeting charges against him and it would be difficult to suggest a better method than a trial based on well tried principles of English law, the juvenile court should not cease to be a court of justice; and secondly,

2. When the offence is really serious and has been proved, it is right that its gravity should be brought home to the offender. In this way a feeling of respect for the law would be strengthened.

By these two statements on policy, the committee set the stamp of approval of what was then, and still is, acceptable, namely that criminal procedure is the fairest way of dealing with a juvenile who comes before the court as a delinquent.

The Committee on Children and Young Persons 1960, the Ingleby Committee (para. 64), though not quite so certain about the propriety of criminal jurisdiction as its predecessor had been, nevertheless stuck to the same principle on the grounds that its strength lay in its being reasonably acceptable to the community because it satisfies the general demand that there should be some defined basis for State intervention.

Apart from dealing with delinquents, the juvenile courts also deal with juveniles who require protection. We noted in the preceding chapter that even before the establishment of the juvenile courts, it had become possible for magistrates' courts to deal judicially with children who had been neglected, cruelly treated or otherwise abused by adults. And the early legislation, which originally covered a comparatively narrow range of circumstances, was gradually added to and amended, notably in 1908, 1933, 1952 and 1963, until today, magistrates in juvenile courts may exercise a wide protective function on a non-criminal basis. In these cases, the child is not charged with an offence, indeed often he is too young to understand the nature of the proceedings, but the court must, to commence with, establish whether the grounds on which their intervention is sought can be substantiated before any decision about the methods of dealing with him can be taken. Both sets of proceedings, criminal and non-criminal, must have a strictly defined legal basis before the court can make any order as to treatment.

Criminal jurisdiction is exercisable over the age group of ten years to seventeen, while non-criminal jurisdiction can be applied to the whole age range up to seventeen years. Apart from noting that sometimes very young children are dealt with by the courts, it would be difficult for a layman to distinguish in practice whether the court is dealing with a case on a criminal or non-criminal basis since the procedure is similar. When it comes to the application of treatment measures, these too are broadly similar, and in some cases, identical, for both categories.

We shall be returning to the position of the application of non-criminal jurisdiction in the juvenile courts later on, because of the part it has played in thinking about changes in policy; but for the remainder of this chapter we shall confine discussion to the position of delinquents alone.

Procedure in juvenile court

It is intended here to present only a basic outline of the
38

procedures as applied to delinquents, since comprehensive descriptions can be found in a number of texts (James, 1962, Chapters 7 and 8; Walker, 1965, Part III [10]). Nevertheless a limited description of them is necessary in order to point out certain of the principles which underlie their use.

Initially one of the objectives for which the juvenile courts were established was that there should be separation of juvenile from adult offenders in order that children should not have to mix with the more experienced older criminals. This, as Rose (1961, p. 86) has commented, was a useful beginning, but no more than that. What was required, but not provided at the outset, was an improvement in the way in which the courts were run and the use of procedures better adapted to the understanding of children. Since those early days, efforts have been directed to securing such improvements. The magistrates of the juvenile court are now selected from a panel, from which they must retire when reaching the age of sixty-five, and the basis of their selection is that they must have a special interest in and understanding of children. The way in which they run their courts is, subject to the uniformly applied statutory rules, left very much to their discretion. The proceedings of the court, as well as the surroundings in which they are conducted, may be more or less formal depending on the magistrates' viewpoint. From what can be gauged through the evidence supplied to the Moloney Committee in 1927, proceedings then often tended to be very formal, which, as the committee noted, 'often presented confusion of thought in the minds of young people', while in later years, one writer noted, matters had undergone a radical change in at least some of the courts in which magistrates had introduced informality to the point of 'softness', when policemen were forbidden to wear their uniforms while attending the proceedings (Jones, 1945, p. 51).

Much of the nature of the proceedings however, is laid down in juvenile court rules formulated by the Home Secretary, which as statutory instruments have the force of law behind them. The salient features of these rules are as follows: the court must explain what the proceedings are about in simple language to the young offender and must allow his parents or a relative to help him in conducting his defence or make statements on his behalf, and if neither parent or relative is present and the child is not legally represented, may go so far as to give him some assistance with the proceedings. In the case of a child up to fourteen years of age, there is no right of trial by jury, but a young person, between fourteen and seventeen has this right when charged with an indictable offence. This must be explained to him so that he may make his choice of trial either by the juvenile court or the appropriate higher court. (In most cases the young person elects to be tried by the former.) The proceedings are not open to the public and attendance at a juvenile court is restricted to those persons who have a direct concern with the case. By this means unnecessary and undesirable embarrassment to the juvenile is avoided. This avoidance of publicity is taken further since in any Press reports and other media for communications to the public, any features by which the juvenile may be identified may not be published. Parents are required to attend the court with their children and if they fail to do so, the magistrates can compel them to come, by this means underlining again the principle of parental responsibility. Considerable stress is also laid on the provision of social reports, and this matter will be considered in a separate section below.

Despite the relaxed atmosphere in which it is considered

proceedings should be conducted, it must be remembered that juvenile courts as at present constituted are essentially courts of law, which means that they must have due regard for substantive law and process. And however well disguised the proceedings may be, a delinquent has to undergo trial for his offence.

The welfare of the child before the court

The modifications in legal procedures relating to juvenile delinquents is bound up with the injunction that the court must have regard for the welfare of every child before it. This concept derived from another of the recommendations of the Moloney Committee. In fact the committee considered that the welfare of the child should be the *primary* object of the juvenile court, but when this suggestion was incorporated in the Children and Young Persons Act 1933, the word *primary* was omitted. Nonetheless, the effect has been that the juvenile court magistrates are directed to attach no undue importance to the nature of the offence, although, as we noted, they must still establish whether or not it was actually committed, and devote at least as much of their attention to the needs of the offender so that they may order suitable treatment.

The introduction of the welfare principle and its adoption in legislation marked an important step forward on the road of progress in relation to the treatment of all children who appear before juvenile courts; but at the same time it raises some discussion about the real function of these courts. One writer (James, 1962, p. 125) recently summarized the problem in the form of a question: 'Juvenile court magistrates are at present in a dilemma as to their functions', he says, and then asks, 'Are they merely judges or do they add to their office the understanding of a child

41

D

therapist?' The answer is that they try and combine both functions and, while by tradition they are considered competent to arbitrate on the issues of guilt and innocence, it has been suggested that their lack of formal training in the fields of psychology or professional social work raises doubt as to their competence to decide on the particular treatment which a child might need. Nor is the welfare of the child the only consideration to which the magistrates must pay regard, apart from adjudicating on the facts of the allegations made. Amongst their other duties there is the need to protect the public from the depredations of juvenile offenders. Therefore a further question to be asked is whether this duty and their duty to have regard to the child's welfare can be reconciled. In the majority of cases with which they deal, the answer would be 'yes'. For where the offence is not a serious one the duty to protect the public is not such an onerous one, and therefore the magistrates may concentrate with a clearer conscience on the type of treatment which the welfare needs of the child calls for. Of considerably greater difficulty is any resolution of problems presented by the commission of serious offences. Dare the magistrates do anything else but to remove, say, the young rapist from his home, though *his* welfare requires a different sort of treatment? Inevitably such cases highlight the conflict which can arise when competing principles call for equal consideration.

The importance of social enquiry

In the Third Report of the Home Office Children's Department, 1925, comment was made that juvenile courts were not served satisfactorily with full information about the young delinquents' backgrounds. The Moloney Committee took up the matter in its discussions and reported that in its opinion it was 'essential that the juvenile court, whose main function [sic] it is to consider the welfare of the young persons who come before it and to prescribe appropriate treatment for them, should have, in all except trivial cases, the fullest information as to the young person's history, his home surroundings and circumstances, his career at school and his medical record.' Following this, the Children and Young Persons Act 1933 made the local authority responsible for rendering relevant information to the juvenile court about any child before it, very much along the lines suggested by the 1927 Committee.

The magistrates rely to a great extent on these reports, for without them, they would have no adequate means of knowing which form of treatment to order. They might, in their absence, place on probation when they should remove from home, or fine when they should make an attendance order. These sorts of decision are obviously better made after a fuller understanding of the child's needs has been reached through the information provided in the reports.

The various sources from which the information is gathered give some indication of the number of agencies and persons which serve the juvenile court. The probation officer, or in some areas, the local authority's child care staff, will report on home surroundings, on the kind of family and neighbourhood the child comes from, and how his parents view the court proceedings. The headmaster of the school will submit a report on educational attainment and behaviour, and there may be medical and psychiatric reports as well. In some cases, where the juvenile has already spent a period in a remand or reception home before the magistrates decide on treatment, there will, in addition, be reports from the superintendent. All this is done to ensure that the court gets a comprehensive picture of the child with whom it has to deal, particularly necessary in those cases where removal from home is indicated. Only the result of social enquiries can enable it to determine which course of action to pursue.

Treatment of young delinquents—general considerations

The care and consideration extended to juveniles, which is evident from the modified procedures already noted, can be seen to a more marked degree in the variety of treatment facilities available to the court. One of the developments which has taken place in this field during the first half of this century has been their greater diversification. As Marshall (1965, p. 1119) has pointed out, there has been a shift in emphasis from the punishment of crime to the promotion of the child's welfare. All the same, punishment in some form still retains its place in treatment. For example, the use of fines is largely a punitive measure and recognized as such by all concerned, and the attendance centre order, while it has some reformatory function, is in the main a form of punishment by depriving a juvenile of his leisure time. There are other forms of treatment which the magistrates will apply because of their training value rather than a means of punishment, but which will appear as punishment to child and parents, especially those measures which involve removal from home. Where, for example, two offenders come before the court, both having committed the same type of offence, perhaps even jointly, and one of them is placed on probation while the other is committed to an approved school, it is doubtful if the latter child would not think that he has been punished while his companion has been 'let off'.

The reasons why, in the case of juveniles, punishment continues to figure amongst the treatment measures, are

44

bound up with social attitudes compounded from a number of motives which cannot be adequately discussed here. All that can be said is that punitive measures do exist, but that their forms change from time to time. Thus, imprisonment of juveniles is practically a thing of the past and birching, once a much used measure, was finally abolished in 1948.

It was mentioned that the range of treatment measures has increased considerably in recent times, but some of the facilities are available only for certain age groups or in respect of certain types of offence. There is a proscription of some of the measures on the grounds that the nature of the offence, statutorily determined, is not serious enough to warrant their use. For example, a juvenile may only be ordered to attend at an attendance centre if he has committed an offence for which, if he were an adult, he could be sent to prison. The same limitation applies to juvenile offenders to be committed to the care of a fit person or an approved school. No juvenile may be sent to a detention centre under the age of fourteen, or to a borstal institution under the age of fifteen. There is also the problem of availability of facilities. They may simply not exist for a particular juvenile court's use, or else it may be impossible to get a placement. For instance, attendance centres, which by their nature must be within reasonable travelling distance of the young delinquent's home, are not available in country areas and therefore attendance centre orders cannot be made in those juvenile courts which serve them (see Walker, 1965, p. 187). Similarly, as is mentioned in the Home Office (1964, p. iv) Children's Department Report for 1961-63, it has happened that the courts have been frustrated from using a certain form of treatment which involves the child's removal from home to a remand home or approved school, because no vacancy could be found

45

owing to a national shortage of such accommodation. It is not sufficient to have a policy which provides for a variety of treatment measures unless adequate resources exist by which that policy can be implemented.

Juvenile court magistrates may apply different measures for the cases before them according to the volume or the nature of delinquency in their particular area. Hence the pattern of treatment ordered can show variations between one area and another. Dr Max Grünhut, in a study of differences in delinquency and treatment methods in England and Wales, made the following comment on this matter: 'Magistrates are likely to consider actual conditions as they prevail in their areas. They are influenced in their outlook by the rise and fall in the number of young offenders and the more serious or more trifling character of the offences they have to deal with'. While he noted that four-fifths of all juveniles in England and Wales lived in areas where the treatment practice of the courts did not differ a great deal from the average, nevertheless, there were considerable variations. In some districts, for instance, magistrates used the probation order much more than in others, while elsewhere they fined more frequently. Apart from this, and leaving aside those situations where statute law places a limit on the age groups for which some measures only may be applied, magistrates may tend themselves to apply some measures more to a given age group rather than others. It was found by Dr Grünhut (1956, pp. 82-3) that on the whole, magistrates favoured probation in the case of older girls, while using orders of absolute discharge more often in the case of younger ones. Older boys were more often committed to approved schools than the younger ones.

We need to bear in mind that, first, types of offence and given age place a limitation on the type of treatment;

second, facilities may exist in theory but not in practice; and third, magistrates may use some facilities more readily than others.

Types of treatment

According to a classification used by Watson (1965, p. 152) treatment facilities may be divided into two broad groupings. The first he describes as 'treatment with the juvenile remaining at home' and the second as 'treatment which involves removal of the juvenile from home.' There are other forms of classification; for example, the Home Office (1965, para. 21-40 and 41-72) distinguishes between 'treatment in the "open" ', and 'institutional treatment', but Watson's method has the merit of drawing a more useful distinction. In the brief survey which follows, and in which the various facilities will be described, Watson's classification will be used.

In the case of a juvenile remaining at home, there will be a minimum of disturbance, since his schooling or employment need suffer no interruption and he will in every case remain under the control of his parents or guardian as the case may be. The measures which may be used consist of the following:

1. *Discharge Order*. A juvenile may be discharged, either absolutely or conditionally. In either event the court will have found the case against him proved, but under an order of absolute discharge no further action on the offence will be taken, whereas under a conditional discharge order, the magistrates may review their decision and impose some other treatment measure if the juvenile commits another offence within a given period, which does not exceed twelve months.

2. *Binding over*. The court may bind over the parents of a juvenile offender, or the juvenile himself, in a sum of money which can be estreated wholly or in part if he commits a further offence. As a rule it is the parent who is called upon to give security for his child's good behaviour for a specified time, and the sum of money involved in the bond could be fixed at as high as £50.

3. *Payment of fines, damages, compensation and costs.* Orders for monetary payments may be made for any or all of these purposes although the total amount which may be imposed is limited by statute. Where children, as distinct from young persons, are dealt with in this way, it is their parents who *must* be made responsible for the payment, while in the case of young persons, the parents *may* be called upon to pay, unless the court is satisfied that they did not in any way contribute to the commission of the offence through their failure to exercise proper care.

4. *Probation (without a condition of residence away from home).* This probation order involves a juvenile being placed under the supervision of a probation officer for a period of up to three years. It is the probation officer's duty to advise, befriend and assist the young delinquent. Probation work has developed in recent years along social casework lines with the central theme of stressing the importance of establishing a good relationship between worker and client. The probationer being the client, the success of the measure in any one case depends very largely on his co-operation. It is for that reason that in the case of a young person, though not of a child, the court may make a probation order only if he consents to it. This emphasises the voluntary aspect of participation and a good deal of mutual trust between probation officer and client.

48

5. *Attendance centre.* Attendance centres were first brought into being through the Criminal Justice Act 1948, although the measure had been thought of and, but for the war years, would have been introduced some ten years earlier. The original aim of these centres was to provide an alternative form of treatment for young offenders not considered to require institutional treatment but who did need something more drastic than probation (see Braithwaite, 1951-52). The Home Office (1965, para. 35) declares the object of the treatment to be 'the vindication of the law by imposing loss of leisure and to bring the delinquent for a period under the influence of representatives of the State'. An order may be made for a total of up to twenty-four hours, although the usual period is for twelve hours, of which not less than one nor more than three hours must be spent at the centre on any one occasion. The centres are run by the police on behalf of the Home Office. A study (McClintock, 1961, p. 99) made on the after-conduct of boys who had undergone this type of treatment has shown that attendance orders are quite effective when applied to young offenders who have little or no experience previously of crime, and who come from a normal home background. They are not so effective when used for the more habitual offenders, particularly those who have previously failed to respond to probation. Since the order means that a young offender has to give up a precious Saturday morning or afternoon over a number of weeks, it is probably not a very palatable proposition for him.

Next we come to the range of measures which involve removal from home. The magistrates may at times be reluctant to take the final step of removing a juvenile from home, but they are in fact bound by statute to do so. The same section (section 44) in the Children and Young Persons Act 1933 which enjoins them to have regard for the welfare

49

of the child or young person, also enjoins them that they must 'in a proper case take steps for removing him from undesirable surroundings and secure that proper provision is made for his education and training'. Hence the need for the residential treatment facilities. These are:

6. *Probation with a condition of residence (Away From Home).* This consists of a probation order that has inserted in it a requirement that the probationer resides in a probation hostel or home or else in lodgings. Such a requirement is usually made when it is thought that it would be best for the young delinquent to move away from home for a time because of his association with undesirable companions or because he needs to develop steady work habits.

7. *Committal to the care of a fit person.* This measure is amongst the earlier established ones since it was first introduced in respect of young delinquents through the Children Act 1908. At that time it was hoped that private individuals, relatives or friends, or voluntary child care organizations would come forward to offer their services, and stand in *loco parentis* to a child whom the court wished to commit to care. But this never proved to be the case to any large extent. So in 1933, again through the Children and Young Persons Act, it became possible for the local authority to act as a fit person and, since the Children Act, 1948, it has in the majority of instances, been its duty, as distinct from a power to act if called upon to do so by the court. In the fit person order, the local authority has the same rights and duties as the parent, and moreover, has a prior right of custody. An advantage often claimed for it is that it enables a child to be placed with foster parents, and so helps him to make a much closer relationship with them than would be possible in the other types of treatment facilities when he has to live away from home.

Most fit person orders are made to the local authority and
since it can provide a wide range of facilities apart from
foster care, it can change a child's treatment according to
need without further referral to the juvenile court. Unless
revoked earlier, an order may remain in existence until the
juvenile's eighteenth birthday.

8. *Detention Centre*. The detention centre order is something that is relatively new in the range of treatment
measures. Like the attendance centre, it was created
through the Criminal Justice Act 1948. When the Bill was
passing through the House of Commons in 1947, the Home
Secretary explained what the government saw the purpose
of the centre to be. 'It provides' he said, 'for the young
offender to whom a fine or a probation order would be
inadequate, but who does not require the prolonged period
of training which is given in an approved school or borstal
institution.' He continued, 'there is a type of offender to
whom it is necessary to give a short, sharp reminder that
he is getting into ways that will inevitably lead him into
disaster' (Hansard, H. C., 1947-48). The Home Office (1965,
para. 63) have since described the regime as 'brisk and
deterrent without being harsh or oppressive'. The detention
centre, however, is not available for those under fourteen
years of age, and the period of treatment is normally not
longer than three months.

9. *Approved school training*. The approved schools, the
modern successors to the old reformatory and industrial
schools, still provide the central core of residential training
and as such are frequently used by the juvenile courts.
One of the features of their administration is that the
majority of them, 93 out of 121 in existence in 1963, are
run by voluntary organizations, some by well-known
societies famous for their other forms of child care, some

by local, *ad hoc* committees, independent of the State. The remaining 28 are run by the children's departments of local authorities. But all of them are subject to rules and regulations made by the Secretary of State. Another feature is that they differ from each other in that they cater for specific age groups and impose differing regimes. There is also a quite advanced system of classification of each juvenile committed to an approved school, so that he may be, at least theoretically, sent to the school most likely to serve his particular needs. Boys and girls between ten and seventeen may be sent to such schools, and while the court cannot specify the length of time that will be spent in a school, this may be up to approximately three years, depending on progress made during training. A further feature of the approved school order is that it provides for a period of supervision following release for two years with an extension for a further year on request by the juvenile. Supervision is usually carried out either by a probation officer or a child care officer of the local authority.

10. *Borstal training.* Although one thinks of borstal training more in terms of its application to young men and women offenders, that is to say, more in relation to the age groups that lie outside the area of discussion in this chapter, it does still come within its scope, as it may now (since 1963) be applied to juveniles who have reached the age of fifteen. The borstal system was first established in 1908 as a special method of corrective training for adolescent offenders, taking its name from the village of Borstal in Kent, the location of the first of these institutions. As in the case of approved school training, committal to borstal is for an indeterminate period, but the maximum length of detention is for two years, with an additional two years of supervision after release. The juvenile

court has no power to commit a juvenile to borstal. This is something that can only be done by a higher court. There is also a system of classification before it is decided to which borstal the young offender shall go, and, as with the approved schools, there is a degree of specialization between the twenty-three borstals for boys and three for girls. Some are of the 'open' and others of the 'closed' variety, the latter providing for the more mature offenders with serious criminal records or those who, it is thought, would be too unstable to be trusted in more open conditions. The emphasis in the borstals is on training to strengthen character and is based on progressive trust demanding increasing personal decision, responsibility and self-control. Unlike the approved schools, borstals are run under the aegis of the Home Office.

11. *Detention in remand home*. Remand homes are more commonly used for the safe custody of delinquents before or between court sittings and act as observation centres to help with social reports for the magistrates. It is still possible in certain circumstances for a young delinquent to be sent there as a punishment. But this measure has never been extensively used, and may become a redundant form of treatment before very long.

12. *Imprisonment*. The use of prisons for young delinquents is now largely a thing of the past. No court may now impose imprisonment on a juvenile under the age of seventeen, but for some very serious offences a court may order detention for a specified period. The Home Secretary directs where this should take place and in practice it begins in an approved school or borstal institution or in a part of a prison set aside specially for juveniles.

Before leaving the description of treatment measures,

53

mention must be made of the power of the juvenile court to send a young delinquent to a hospital or place him under guardianship if satisfied, on medical evidence, that he suffers from mental illness or subnormality to a degree which warrants treatment.

General discussion

Walker (1965, pp. 202-3) noted that in 1961 more than every third child and every fourth young person found guilty of an indictable offence was discharged absolutely or conditionally by the magistrates. Of the other measures that were applied, the probation order was the single one most used, followed by the fine. Absolute and conditional discharge, probation order and fine, accounted for the disposal of more than 80% of indictable offences dealt with in the juvenile courts. Of the remaining cases, about 5% of juveniles were sent to attendance centres, about 7% to approved schools, and the remaining 8% were dealt with by being committed to the care of fit persons, sent to detention centres or borstals or dealt with under hospital or guardianship orders. Institutional treatment is therefore reserved for a relatively small proportion of all juvenile delinquents.

The nature of the treatment may differ considerably according to type. Where it is punitive it may call for immediate redress, as in the case of the pecuniary penalties. It may be spread out over a number of weeks as in the case of attendance centre orders, or it may take the form of the 'short sharp shock' provided by the detention centre. Treatment which involves any form of training or guidance is thought of in terms of a longer time-span, and does not necessarily include removal from home. In the case of probation without a condition of residence, it may

54

continue for as long as three years, although two years are usually considered sufficient. A fit-person order could remain effective for many years, depending on the age of the juvenile at the time of the court appearance, since the order does not automatically expire until the age of eighteen years has been reached. Approved school and borstal training also spread over a number of years combining detention with supervised freedom.

All the different types of treatment have at least one objective in common: that through their application in any particular case, the young delinquent's reappearance before a juvenile court can be averted. But when one considers the state of reconviction rates, there is little evidence which suggests that one type is superior to another. Current research in this area may give some help in the future and provide the necessary guidance to the magistrates who must select the specific treatment most likely to be effective in given circumstances.

Conclusion

From the discussion in this chapter, it will have become evident that social policy has been directed toward relaxation of formal procedures in juvenile courts and the provision of a wide range of treatment measures, a process which has evolved gradually over the course of generations, and even so the final word on this subject has by no means been said. Social policy changes, and what seemed appropriate only a short time ago may no longer be so when viewed against the background of changing social needs. One may therefore expect a continuing reappraisal of policies for dealing with young delinquents. We are currently at the height of discussions about fundamental ways of approaching this problem, all stemming from the desire to prevent juvenile delinquency from occurring at all. It is now some forty years since the Moloney Committee on Young Offenders remarked, somewhat wistfully perhaps, that it had been charged with considering methods of 'cure rather than prevention' and thought 'that in the development and strengthening of educational measures greater hope lay in reducing juvenile offences than could be derived from any improvement in curative measures.' This theme has been increasingly receiving attention since, more particularly in the post-war years.

Whether or not the relaxation of formality in legal proceedings, the widening of the range of treatment facilities and the attempt to match treatment itself with the needs of the individual juvenile has had an overall beneficial effect in reducing the extent of delinquency, would be a difficult matter to assess. What can be said with some conviction is that the more liberal and humane methods of dealing with juvenile delinquents over the past fifty years or so have helped to foster, in those concerned in administration of treatment, a more understanding attitude toward the problem involved. This augurs well for the next phase of development.

4
The development of a
preventive service

The growth in juvenile delinquency

Since 1908, when the official machinery for dealing with
juvenile delinquents became firmly established, successive
governments have seen no cause to make any radical
changes in its operations. The Moloney Committee in
reviewing the system, came to the conclusion that 'the
juvenile court was the tribunal best fitted to deal with all
offences other than those which can suitably be met with
a warning', and this statement served to confirm what then
had long been thought of as the right and proper way of
dealing with young delinquents.

Whatever its merits, and the system had many, compared
with what had previously been practice, there could be no
cause for complacency and no cause for thinking that its
methods were specially effective for reducing or even stab-
ilizing the juvenile crime rate. This increased steadily in the
thirties but with a small and short-lived drop just before the
outbreak of the second world war. The figures at that time
however look comparatively innocuous when matched
against the post-war increase and the table below gives an

indication of this comparison in the case of indictable offences.

JUVENILES FOUND GUILTY OF INDICTABLE OFFENCES PER 100,000 OF POPULATION IN AGE/SEX GROUP

Year	Boys 8-17 Years	Girls 8-17 Years
1938	918	62
1948	1587	152
1957	1352	110
1963	1880	215

The steep rise of crime during the war and immediate post-war years, has been attributed to the serious dislocation of social and family life of those years, and false hope was raised when there appeared a reasonable drop in the early fifties. This has not been maintained.

The government was seriously disturbed by the post-war figures and the subject of juvenile crime prompted a debate in the House of Lords in November 1948. Following this, the Home Secretary and the Minister of Education jointly initiated a central conference with the intention of bringing together at national level representatives of all the interests immediately concerned. Later the ministries sent an appropriate memorandum to all chairmen of county councils and mayors of boroughs recommending them to set up their own conferences so that the problems might be studied at local level, and any preventive and remedial measures which seemed necessary to meet the needs of their areas might be taken. The local authorities' response was encouraging: in 1950, a report to the House of Lords (Home Office, 1951, p. 146; also Chapter IV; Appendix X) showed that 88 out of 145 had studied the problem and made some recommendations but when their findings and suggestions were analysed centrally, the two ministries expressed disappointment with the result and led the Home Office to comment that 'while much useful information was collected, many of the reports concentrated on general causes associated popularly with juvenile delinquency rather than on specific local conditions and the application of local remedies' (Home Office, 1955, para. 181; Appendix IX summarises comments on the joint circular, April 1949). Nonetheless it was at least a useful method of gauging informed opinion.

The practice of convening national and local conferences for the discussion of ways and means of preventing delinquency has continued. Although it could not be said that this method is likely to throw much light on the causes, it has the merit of helping to mobilize interest in a problem which clearly should be the concern of as wide a section of the community as possible and, as some recent experience has shown, it can result in the establishment at local level of schemes which have prevention as their main objective. Thus Cardiff set up a 'Parents' Advisory Service' in 1963 throughout the city with the aim of providing a source of guidance, information and help for all parents. In Blackburn and Accrington, as a result of a local conference, a police juvenile liaison service was brought into operation.

The term 'prevention' in the context of juvenile delinquency may be given two meanings. It may be used to describe situations in a family in which circumstances are such that delinquency might arise unless an improvement can be effected through the intervention of a social work agency. It may also be used to describe situations where delinquency is already known to have occurred, and where measures are applied to prevent further offences being committed.

An American writer (Kahn, 1963, pp. 60-65) has distinguished between three levels at which preventive measures may be applied: the ultimate, the intermediate and the immediate. At the ultimate level, the local community interposes itself between the general social environment and the family or the individual, not to prevent specifically delinquency but rather to avoid a breakdown of values. The focus remains on the whole community, on all families, not only those in which delinquency occurs or threatens. At the intermediate level, the local community tries by various means, such as educational or recreational programmes, to raise the cultural aspirations of members of underprivileged groups. The immediate level, which merges with the intermediate, focuses attention specifically on families which are known to be under special social or economic pressure or are considered to be particularly likely to break down, but whose members are not necessarily known to be delinquent.

It is largely with this latter group and therefore the immediate level of prevention that recent discussion in this country has been concerned.

Use of the Social services

It may seem paradoxical that juvenile delinquency should have increased in recent years in view of the expansion of the educational and social services provisions which, the Moloney Committee had hoped, would provide of themselves the best means of reducing it. This is not entirely because of limitations in the extent and quality of services provided (though this aspect must be taken into consideration), but also because the services have not always been applied at the point and time where they would prove most beneficial. In addition the increased provision of social services will tend to uncover social needs and may indirectly provide more work for the juvenile courts. This is particularly true in the case of the community social services.

Many of our social services are concerned with financial provisions. Old age pensions, sickness and unemployment benefits, family allowances and widows' pensions, provide a measure of minimum financial security in circumstances which may happen to anyone at some time or other during their lifetime. Whilst they have not eradicated poverty, for poverty is a relative concept, not an absolute one, they have granted a standard of living for substantial sections of the community which is much higher than that of previous generations.

In addition there are the other community social services which either directly or indirectly have made a very real contribution to the fuller enjoyment of life. Health and welfare services, housing and many others, some reaching every section of the population, some only those people who have a special kind of handicap, have between them raised the standard of living. Despite these beneficial social provisions, juvenile delinquency has been a constant problem. Instead of fading into insignificance it has increased to substantial proportions. If it might be thought that some vital part, some essential service was still missing, this was something which the Ingleby Committee took into account in their examination of the existing services, but it came to the conclusion that there was no need for any new kind of service. Those that existed were potentially well equipped to combat delinquency. What was required was that the various facets of the social services should be brought together and be used more effectively at the time when a family might need them, so that by co-ordination of the services, whether supplied by central or local government departments, hardship could be alleviated and problems of child neglect and delinquency reduced. The committee saw the primary problem as that of ensuring that the existing social services should work together harmoniously.

The background to the idea of prevention of delinquency

We noted in 1927 the Moloney Committee was very much alive to the need for *preventing* delinquency and not only to supplying curative, or treatment measures. At that time educational and welfare services were not nearly as well developed as they are now, but the beginnings were already there, and it was hoped that as facilities expanded, the services would gradually take care of the preventive aspects. This hope has not been fulfilled. Services have expanded, but it is evidently not just a matter of providing the services but also of bringing them to the families at the time when they are needed. This means that families in need must be sought out, for, as social workers can testify, people in need often do not know what services are available, which agency provides them and how help might be applied for. Furthermore, it is accepted that many of the problems now facing families are not of a material nature, but rather problems of personal relationships and inability to cope with the demands made by society about acceptable patterns of child-rearing. So, in order to meet this need, we have seen the development of casework services which, it is hoped, will play a major part in the prevention of delinquency by reducing family tensions, modifying adverse inter-personal relationships between husband and wife or parents and child and, through general support of the

62

family, strike at what is believed to be among the root causes of juvenile delinquent behaviour, namely poor family relationships.

Initially, official encouragement to undertake preventive work came, not so much in relation to juvenile delinquency, but in relation to child cruelty and neglect. Problems associated with these matters had of course been recognized and, to some extent, legislated for since the second half of the last century, but the experience of the evacuation schemes during the second world war forced the government and the public to pay them renewed attention. Evacuation revealed the widespread squalor and degradation under which many children had been living, especially in the large cities, and to which they were likely to return. Considerable disquiet was caused through the revelations about the most serious of the cases, which soon became known as 'problem families', and which one medical officer of health later defined as 'those families who have not responded to the general improvement in social conditions, who are unable by their own efforts to raise their standards and homes to a reasonable level and who have failed to make full use of the social services of which they are in need' (Scott, 1956). It was found that in these families child neglect was common, not necessarily because parents were deliberately cruel or neglectful, but rather through ignorance or sheer inability to cope with life. Studies such as T. Stephen's *Problem Families* (1947), the Women's Group on Public Welfare's *The Neglected Child and his Family* (1948) and R. C. Wolfinden's *Problem Families in Bristol* (1950) did much to focus attention on a serious social problem and pinpointed the difficulties under which certain families lived.

Impressed by the evidence put forward and prodded by a debate in Parliament on the subject in 1949, the Government began to take some action. After a working party from the three ministries most directly concerned, the Ministries of Health, Education and the Home Office, had been set up to study the problem, it was decided not to seek any new legislation, nor indeed to set up any formal commission of enquiry, but rather to circularize local authorities, urging them to take prompt action to bring together all the available community resources to *prevent* the neglect or ill-treatment of children in their own homes. A joint ministerial circular was therefore sent out in 1950 in which a positive recommendation was made for each county council or county borough to establish co-odinateing machinery so designed as to get all the various parts of the social services, statutory as well as voluntary, working together, so that they would be used effectively at the point where a family in need would best benefit from them. The local authorities' response was good. Most of them did set up co-ordinating committees made up of representatives of the various statutory social service departments and voluntary organizations. The task which they set themselves was that of identifying families likely to be at risk and pooling resources in order to provide the necessary support, but the Ingleby Committee (1960, para. 37) later noted that the results of the committees' work were patchy, spoiled too often by inter-departmental rivalries which, not surprisingly, militated strongly against helping the families in question. But a start had been made, and in 1952, the idea of preventive work received a notable impetus when the Select Committee on Estimates, which had examined the child-care service, urged on the grounds of lower costs that more attention should be given to preventing family break-up and so reducing the number of children having to be received into public care (Parker, 1965, p. 50).

In the same year, a useful beginning was made towards

the identification of those families in which child neglect or cruetlty might be occurring when, by an amendment to the Children and Young Persosn Act 1933, the local authority children's departments were given the responsibility for investigating all cases in which children were believed to be in need of care or protection.

The time seemed ripe for a fuller examination of the administrative and other problems involved; and the suggestion that more precise statutory definition might be needed to enable the local authorities to set up full scale preventive services played a part in the decision to set up the Ingleby Committee on Children and Young Persons in 1956. Consequently a part of the committee's terms of reference was concerned with investigating 'whether local authorities responsible for child care ... in England and Wales should, taking into account action by voluntary organizations and the responsibilities of existing statutory services, be given new powers and duties to prevent or forestall the suffering of children through neglect in their own homes.' The recommendation which the committee made on this point read that: 'There should be a general duty laid upon local authorities to prevent or forestall the suffering of children through neglect in their own homes and local authorities should have power to do preventive casework and to provide material needs that cannot be met from other sources.' The committee had not been able to decide which of the local authority departments should have the responsibility for providing the service, and therefore suggested that the powers should be vested generally in the local authority.

The government accepted without reservation the premise of a preventive service and took the view that the functions involved were a natural extension of the work already exercisable by the local authorities' children's departments. It therefore allocated the newly devised statutory duties specifically to them rather than to the local authorities generally. Furthermore they took the opportunity of widening the scope of the preventive work service; for when their policy was later expressed in legislation, in Section 1 of the Children and Young Persons Act 1963, it was specified that preventive work could be applied in any situation in which children might otherwise have to be received into care, or brought before the juvenile court, no mention being made that this might be restricted to those cases where child neglect or cruelty was the matter in issue. Later a Home Office memorandum (No. 22/1964) made it clear that the provisions covered any contingency which could bring a child before the juvenile court. Since 1963, then, children's departments have been charged with the special duty to provide advice, guidance and assistance to families so as to prevent delinquency as well as child neglect. In fact the provision makes good sense, since there is evidence that child neglect and juvenile delinquency are often found linked in the same family (Wilson, 1962, p. 146).

Children's Departments have been placed in the forefront of this area of social work, but are not the only agencies now active in it; the police in a number of districts also have special schemes, their juvenile liaison services; and other agencies such as the probation, and child guidance as well as the youth service, have for many years been involved in the prevention of juvenile delinquency. Preventive work is by no means a monopoly possessed by one particular social work agency but, since it is the first two departments whose particular contribution has been engaging most discussion within the last few years, we shall devote a separate section to describing the part played by each of them.

Local authority Children's Departments

Until 1948 the public care of children was, in the main, the responsibility of public assistance committees, local education authorities and local health authorities. Circumstances which resulted in children coming into care arose through the death of parents, serious illness, desertion, imprisonment, homelessness and similar causes. These children would generally be the responsibility of the public assistance committee. Other circumstances, such as a child's delinquency or parental neglect, might result in committal to the local education authority. Then there were situations in which parents might be unable to look after their children for a temporary period, for instance through the mother's confinement or illness, which could result in such children being cared for by the local health authority.

In 1945 a great deal of disquiet over the quality of care was expressed through the medium of the Press, and this led to the government setting up an inter-departmental committee of enquiry, under the chairmanship of Miss (later Dame) Myra Curtis. This committee reported only eighteen months later, and the most important of its recommendations involved a drastic administrative reorganization of existing child-care functions. The recommendation was that each county council and county borough council should establish a new children's committee to deal exclusively with all the child-care functions previously carried out by the other departments mentioned above. This was accepted by the government, and the resultant Children Act 1948 created the modern children's committees and departments. Their first major task was to concentrate efforts on methods of care, in particular to disband the large barrack-like children's homes, a legacy of poor law days, and to extend the system of fostering as advocated in the Curtis Committee report.

As in the case of the delinquency services, the new child care service's function lay in the improvement of methods of care. But the staff of the department concerned with the fieldwork quickly became aware that in many of the cases which they were called upon to deal with, children could have been *prevented* from coming into care. The Children Act had not made preventive work explicit and there was doubt as to how far resources could be expended by the new committees on this type of activity. All the same, it was soon found that it was unrealistic to divide work neatly into care activities and preventive functions and as time went on, in the absence of official disapproval, more and more local authorities began to undertake preventive work quite openly. The Home Office (1955, paras. 5-11), which, at central level had been made responsible for the local authorities' child care functions, recognized that the Children Act was silent on the matter of authorizing expenditure on preventive work, and therefore did its best by urging them to apply those preventive facilities which existed under other social service provisions against child neglect and family break-up. So far as the children's departments were concerned, they did use those resources, adding them to their own, and generally took a liberal view in interpreting all the statuory powers which they had at their disposal in order to apply preventive measures over as wide a front as their limited resources permitted.

This type of work had already become an established function when the Ingleby Committee enquired into existing powers. What the resultant legislations did was to strengthen the Children's Departments' hands by explicitly enabling them to expend money on preventive work, recruit additional staff to carry it out, and set up specific sub-departments to carry out supportive family casework designed to prevent children having to come into care for any reason including delinquency.

Another aspect of the work of the Children's Departments which is relevant to the subject matter under discussion here concerns the way in which services for delinquent and non-delinquent children have developed in this country. Children labelled delinquent or in need of protection may be committed to the care of the local authority, acting in its capacity of fit person, while others come into care for a variety of reasons without the intervention of the courts. But once they are under the umbrella of public care, there can be no distinction in the manner of treatment whatever the legal grounds for admission were that brought them there. The important point is that the distinction is lost *after* and not *before* the children arrive in care. The two main routes up to that stage remain, one taking the route via the court, the other by-passing it. We noted in a previous context that it may be chance that brings one child before the court as delinquent and another as requiring care, protection or control. So it is equally often chance which results in one child being *received* into care at the request of a parent while another is *committed* by a court to the care of the local authority.

Police juvenile liaison schemes

It is appropriate to single out the liaison schemes for a brief descriptive account as they are specifically designed to reduce the number of young offenders who might otherwise come before the juvenile court.

The first of these schemes was initiated in Liverpool in 1949. Their spread throughout England and Wales since that date has however not been as fast as one might have expected, since not every chief officer of police is necessarily in favour of them. In 1964 twelve out of the 117 police authorities had established such a service.

The Liverpool scheme has served as the model and is the one which has featured in various reports and journals from time to time (see Ingleby Committee, 1960, paras. 139-149; Kilbrandon Committee, 1964, paras. 149-50; Liverpool, 1962; Mack, 1962-63; Mays, 1965). It was based on the normal police practice of cautioning an offender instead of resorting to prosecution. The use of cautioning young offenders after minor offences have been committed is itself an old-established procedure, but there had never been any attempt to follow it up on an organized basis, and a valuable opportunity was lost for keeping in contact with an offender whose offence, however trivial, might conceivably have led to more serious crime. The police of course use their discretion in supplying cautions and, as one writer has recently said, 'the liaison officer scheme is the logical outcome of established cautionary and preventive functions' (Mays, 1965, p. 186). In the Liverpool scheme, the aim is to establish contact between either delinquent or potential delinquent and a specially selected police officer. The essence of contact involves the co-operation of parents as much as child, and enlisting the help of all the educational and social services which operate in the city. Participation is entirely voluntary and the service is not offered as an alternative to prosecution. It is interesting to note that at the outset it was the actual rather than the potential delinquent who was being dealt with, but the proportion of the latter category has risen considerably.

Reaction to the scheme has been mixed. The official viewpoint has been favourable, though not to the extent of
70

THE DEVELOPMENT OF A PREVENTIVE SERVICE

recommending compulsory operation in all areas of the country. After the Advisory Council on the Treatment of Offenders had considered the workings of the Liverpool scheme soon after its inception, the Home Secretary expressed his approval of it to Parliament in 1954, stating that he believed it to be a 'sound method of dealing with incipient juvenile delinquency' and that he wanted to see its adoption in other suitable areas (Home Office, 1955, para. 188). On the other hand, the Ingleby Committee (1960, para. 147), whilst conceding that it was impressed by what it had heard of the results, was not sure that such work should be undertaken by the police. The main objection was that it involved the exercise of casework skills of a nature which police officers were not qualified to carry out.

Since that time, official policy has been one of treading cautiously. There has certainly been no sign of an enthusiastic plunge into a practice which, while it promises much, is beset by a number of difficulties; doubts about the propriety of using the police for such a function, the use of untrained personnel, and the admitted lack of systematically collected evidence of the measure of success, being amongst them. In the meantime, individual police authorities continue their experiments with them.

Conclusion

In this chapter we have been considering two aspects: the steep rise in the juvenile delinquency figures in the years following the last war, and the interest which has been taken in the measures designed to arrest and if possible, reverse the trend. In one way it may be argued that it is of little value to concentrate resources on prevention of delinquency when there is only a hazy notion about its causation. There is of course much truth in such an assertion, but in fairness it should be pointed out that this is a matter that has not escaped official notice. While effort is being directed to devising and encouraging new ideas in preventive work, the government is also initiating and furthering research concerned with finding out about treatment measures and crime causation (Home Office, 1964, see the section headed 'Research'). In the meantime there is a general presumption that a great deal of the causation of crime lies rooted in social forces about whose workings we know all too little. This being so, it follows that any preventive work undertaken at this stage of our knowledge can be only tentative and largely experimental.

One interesting factor however is emerging about the approach used in preventive work. In all its forms there is a concentration of effort on the family as a whole rather than on the individual delinquent or potential delinquent in isolation from his family. The co-operation of the whole family is actively sought in finding ways and means of preventing delinquency, and by providing positive support from official sources there is a good opportunity of under-pinning the strength of the primary social unit in our society.

The last century marked progress in the treatment of the young delinquent by moving away from the principle of retribution to that of reform through education and training. This came about by a radical rethinking of policy and reshaping of penal measures. In this century, so far, we have witnessed a greater emphasis on meeting individual needs, and consequently a greater diversification of treatment measures. Now, we have arrived at the time when a further departure from traditional thinking about the treatment of juvenile delinquents is under discussion.

5
Rethinking social policy

Introduction

When the juvenile court system was first established at the beginning of this century, its prime objective was to separate the administration of the criminal law between juveniles and adults. In achieving this objective it has proved successful. For many years the system had remained unassailed, and it received the support of two government committees of enquiry, separated from each other in time by a generation, so that it might be thought that the last word on the subject had been said. But there is always the possibility that the juvenile court system, created as a means to an end, could become an end in itself. Like any other formal institution, it has the tendency to become self-protective because of vested interests in its perpetuation. During the course of its development it has grown in prestige and power. Among the personnel who serve the court, the juvenile court magistrates have important status in the community, being regarded as persons of some standing because of their functions. Probation officers too have a considerable investment in juvenile court work, taking a

73

major share in the social enquiry aspects as well as acting as supervisors of the large numbers of boys and girls who are placed on probation. It is therefore quite likely that the system would continue if only because the personnel most directly concerned in it have a very real interest in its continuance and are unlikely of themselves to abdicate from their established positions unless they are dissatisfied about its purpose or efficacy; and this, for the most part, is not the case. But an even more important factor is that of the ideology which underlines the system. Because it is deeply rooted in the traditional grounds of justice, hallowed by time, it is well placed to resist any attempt to change it radically. Those changes that have been made over the years have served to strengthen the structure rather than weaken it.

For all that, the juvenile court system has been challenged quite recently. Indeed it has gone beyond the stage of challenge, for the government has put forward proposals to break with tradition, to abolish the juvenile courts altogether and instead to adopt a system in which procedures will be essentially non-judicial. Not surprisingly these proposals have aroused strong opposition, not only as might be expected, from magistrates and probation officers who are closely associated with the work, but from other quarters where the threat of abandoning the traditional system is seen both as a departure from established principles of justice and as a possibility of placing a premium on lawlessness.

Before examining the new proposals in some detail, we shall consider certain of the findings of the two committees of enquiry, one for England and Wales and the other for Scotland, which within a few years of each other, were charged with considering the appropriateness of the juvenile court system for this day and age. We have already

74

made reference to one of these, the Ingleby Committee, in connection with the discussion on preventive work, and now we must turn again to its findings to note what it had to say about juvenile courts, in particular about the treatment of juvenile delinquents who come before those courts. The other committee to be referred to is Ingleby's equivalent for Scotland, the Committee on Children and Young Persons (Scotland) 1964, often referred to as the Kilbrandon Committee. The approach of this committee is similar to that of the government's plans in the White Paper *The Child, the Family and the Young Offender* and to the proposals of other study groups and individuals whose views we shall also note.

The Ingleby Committee's recommendations 1961

There was little doubt in the committee members' minds that the only acceptable way for dealing with young delinquents was through the juvenile courts because of the judicial nature of the proceedings which protected the rights of the individual. It did however concede that certain changes were desirable so long as these took place within the judicial system. The committee felt some misgivings about the nature of the criminal proceedings to which children were subject and the conflict which this engendered with the provision that the court must have regard for the welfare of every child who appeared before it. This, the committee said in its report:

> had produced a jurisdiction that rests on principles that are hardly consistent. The court remains a criminal court in the sense that it is a magistrates' court that is principally concerned with trying offences, that its procedure is a modified form of ordinary criminal procedure and that with a few special provisions, it is governed by the

75

law of evidence in criminal cases. Yet the requirement to have regard for the welfare of the child, and the various ways in which the court may deal with an offender, suggests a jurisdiction that is not criminal. It is not easy to see how the two principles can be reconciled: criminal responsibility is focused on an allegation about some particular act isolated from the character and needs of the defendant, whereas welfare depends on a complex of personal, family and social consideration (Ingleby Committee, 1960, para. 60).

Having made this statement the committee clearly found itself in a dilemma. On one hand it had already declared for the juvenile court system and hence the judicial procedure; on the other, the welfare principle was inviolable. In the event, a compromise solution was recommended in that the category of children who come before the court on the basis of requiring care of protection should be enlarged by adding to it children up to twelve years of age, (later, it was hoped, to be extended to the fourteen-year-olds) who had hitherto been dealt with as delinquents. Such children could still be brought before the court, but for protective reasons, being in need of some form of discipline rather than as delinquents. In effect, the recommendations on this point meant that the age of criminal responsibility would be raised to twelve years and a child under that age would no longer be liable to criminal prosecution and conviction. Of course, this would not mean that he could not commit offences, but the law would prescribe a new way in which he should come before the court. The reasoning behind this change in procedures for the younger age groups explains the addition of the word 'control' to the long-used phrase 'care or protection' since this provision would, in future, cover not only children who were neglected, endangered and beyond parental control, but also those who committed offences.

This suggested line of action followed previous developments, for the category of children who were considered to be in need of care or protection has been steadily enlarged ever since the beginning of the century. The latest group to be added to it would be children under twelve who had committed offences. To make certain that there would be no diminution in a young offender's sense of personal responsibility for his actions the committee added the recommendation that the court should have power to order detention in a remand home or attendance at an attendance centre for any child found to be in need of care, protection or control, a power which had not previously been available for care or protection cases because these types of treatment were primarily punitive in nature.

So no radical recommendations were forthcoming from this committee. For some children (about 13,500 boys and girls between the ages of eight and twelve years who were found guilty of all types of offences during the course of a year) care, protection or control proceedings might be substituted for criminal proceedings. So far as any social stigma attaches to criminal proceedings, this would be removed for these children; but so far as this stigma attaches to the court appearance itself, it would remain.

Doubt had for some years been expressed in informed quarters about the minimum age of criminal responsibility. There was a feeling that it was fixed at too low an age level, and indeed the thought of an eight-or nine-year-old having to defend himself in cross examination against an adult prosecutor made for sober reflection. But if the Ingleby Committee's proposals on this matter might be considered modest enough, the government of the day was most reluctant to accept them. As things stood, fines and the probation order could be used in the case of such young offenders, but 'if the age of criminal responsibility were to be raised it would be impossible for the courts to deal with youthful delinquents in those salutory ways', Lord Dilhorne, the Lord Chancellor, commented, when the proposal to raise the age limit for criminal proceedings came up for debate as part of the Children and Young Persons Bill in the House of Lords in December 1962 (Hansard, H. L., 1962b). But the onslaught of the opposition to gain this modification was fierce, and the outcome was a compromise solution in that the minimum age of criminal responsibility was fixed at ten years.

All in all the Ingleby Committee had done little more than recommend a few, mostly minor, alterations to the juvenile court system for dealing with young delinquents. Those who had expected more from the committee, which had been deliberating for four years, were disappointed. Lady Wootton expressed the feelings of those who had hoped for much more when she said: 'We had been hoping for a bold and imaginative reconstruction of the whole system for dealing with unfortunate and delinquent children in this day and age. What we got was a number of useful minor reforms on a system which, in the judgement of many of us, is already outmoded' (Hansard, H. L., 1962a). The government however was quite content to hold to traditional practice and in no way inclined to depart from it.

What the Ingleby Committee was not prepared to suggest for England and Wales and the government did not want in any case, the Kilbrandon Committee was imaginative enough to offer to Scotland.

The Kilbrandon Committee's recommendations

Four years after the Ingleby Committee had made its report

78

on the situation in England, the Kilbrandon Committee, charged with a similar task although not dealing with preventive aspects as such, did the same for Scotland. The juvenile court system had not developed there in the way as it had in England. In particular it was not so uniformly spread throughout the country. The basic problem which faced the Scottish committee was however the same that the Ingleby Committee had to consider, namely whether the existing juvenile court system was the most suitable that could be devised to meet the needs of delinquent as well as neglected children. And the Kilbrandon Committee, unlike its English counterpart, was not satisfied that it was the most suitable. It did not think that any form of judicial procedure was the best way of going about meeting the needs of children, which it believed were mainly educational and social in nature. In any case, it argued, so far as delinquents were concerned, the necessity for formal and criminal proceedings hardly applied when experience had shown that in the large majority of cases, 95%, the facts in the allegations were not in dispute and in the few cases where they were, provisions for judicial hearing could always be devised.

In the light of this, the committee recommended that all juveniles under the age of sixteen years, whether delinquent or in need of care or protection, should in future be brought before a specially created agency, to be called the juvenile panel, whose sole concern would be the measures to be applied on what amounts to an agreed referral. Provided the child and parent agreed that the allegation as to acts committed was true, the agency would then proceed to deal with the child. If there was a denial, then the case would be refered to the Sheriff Court, which, if it found the allegation to be substantiated, would refer the case back to the agency for applying treatment measures.

79

Such an agency would clearly not be a criminal court of law, or indeed a court in any accepted sense. It would be the duly constituted public agency authorized to deal with juvenile offenders, where necessary by the application of compulsory measures (Kilbrandon Committee, para. 73). It is of interest to note that the juvenile panel would be a public agency, not only independent of the court, but also independent of the local authorities, in no way subservient to either, and composed essentially of a lay body of persons who either by knowledge or experience were deemed specially qualified to consider children's problems.

The major thesis in the Kilbrandon Report was the need for emphasis to be laid on the treatment of delinquent children rather than the proving of facts in allegations. Because of this, the committee rejected outright the concept of criminal proceedings and with it the continued use of the juvenile courts. The compromise solution which the Ingleby Committee had suggested, namely that of reducing the scope of criminal proceedings while enlarging that of care or protection proceedings, albeit within the juvenile court system, did not appeal to the Kilbrandon Committee because the emphasis would still be primarily on the proof of facts rather than assessment of needs, and the only real change would be in the nomenclature of the proceedings used.

This brief summary of the relevant parts of the Scottish report has been brought into the discussion here to show that realistic alternatives to the juvenile court system were being put forward in one part of the British Isles at a time when, in another part, they were being turned down and not contemplated as official policy. But the debate about alternatives had begun in England too, only a short time after the Kilbrandon Committee had issued its report. Two and a half years later in October 1966 the Secretary of

State for Scotland presented proposals to Parliament for the recasting of the system in that country for dealing with delinquent children and others under the age of sixteen who require some form of care or control or who behave in other specified seriously anti-social ways. The recommendations of the Kilbrandon Committee are followed closely in this White Paper called 'Social Work and the Community', namely that suitable cases would go before a panel of lay people served by an official to be known as the 'Reporter'. He would have responsibility for making the initial decision whether a child appears to be in trouble or difficulty acting on information supplied by the police and other sources. This new service would work in conjunction with a new local authority service, the social work department, which would gather together from existing departments services for children, probation work, both for children and adults, community care and after care of the ill, welfare of handicapped persons and old people, domestic help provisions and temporary accommodation for homeless families.

It is considered in the White Paper that many of the cases which the panel would otherwise deal with could be filtered off through timely help by the social work department. The panel is not envisaged as acting as a persuasive agency only, relying entirely on co-operation from parents but will be empowered to *order* treatment and training for a child if the parents do not voluntarily agree to it. The panel might be seen by some as the juvenile court in another guise but the emphasis will be on welfare needs rather than a preoccupation with the establishment of facts in issue, though to be sure, the safeguard of recourse to a court by the child is preserved.

The Longford proposals

In June 1964 the Labour Party published a report called *Crime: A Challenge to Us All*, which contained the outcome of the discussions and recommendations of a study group led by Lord Longford. In this report there were, amongst other matters, proposals about new ways of dealing with juvenile delinquents. Since this was a Labour Party publication, the chances were that the party, if it came to power, would translate these proposals, or something very much like them, into official policy.

The study group had been set up by Mr Harold Wilson to advise the Labour Party on matters concerning the prevention of crime and the improvement and modernization of penal practice. A substantial part of the report was devoted to the discussion of juvenile delinquency. In this respect, the group's proposals included provisions for, first, 'the establishment of a family service with the aim of helping every family to provide for its children the careful nurture and attention to individual and social needs that the fortunate majority already enjoy, and, secondly changes in judicial procedure which will take children of school age out of the range of the criminal courts and the penal system and treat their problems in a family setting, where necessary through family courts' (Longford Study Group, p. 1).

The setting up of a family service had been the subject of discussion in a number of official reports as well as in social work circles for some time, and had already been agreed in principle in many quarters. In broad terms, the aim is to bring together the currently fragmented parts of the community social services which impinge closely on family welfare, such as those provided by parts of the

82

health, welfare and education departments of the local authority, as well as the children's departments, placing them under one composite administration. The advantages of a family service would be considerable, allowing for better overall planning, better use of scarce skilled manpower resources and, one would hope, a lessening of those inter-departmental rivalries in the local-authority-provided social services which tend to detract from the value of the work, and which had already been the subject of disapproving comment by the Ingleby Committee. There was therefore nothing in this first proposal which was likely to arouse substantial disagreement. But in the second, there was the quite categorical proposal to abandon the juvenile court system in dealing with young delinquents, and this was likely to prove a much more controversial issue.

More particularly, the Longford recommendations on this point were as follows: delinquent children under the age of thirteen years would in future be dealt with by the family service when a case had been brought to its attention by either the police, school or whatever agency had first been made aware of it. Each local authority would have its own family service and this would decide on the kind of treatment necessary. An important feature of the scheme would be the emphasis on close co-operation with the child's parents and their agreement to any form of treatment would be essential. In cases where agreement could not be reached, the matter would be referred to a family court, a judicial agency to be newly established, which would handle these cases as well as other matters such as care, protection or control cases of juveniles up to the age of seventeen, hear criminal charges against boys and girls between fifteen and eighteen years old, and deal with a number of other social issues affecting not only juveniles, but also adults such as, for instance, matrimonial matters. Delinquent children between thirteen years old and school-leaving age would also be dealt with directly by the family service, so long as their parents agreed to this procedure, in the same way as younger children. In cases of serious delinquency, it would be open to the family service or the police to bring a child who was still below school-leaving age, directly before the family court on the basis of care, protection or control proceedings.

The study group's philosophy which underlies these proposals is best summarized from this quotation in its report:

> We believe that in justice to our children, and for the health and well being of society, no child in early adolescence should have to face criminal proceedings: these children should receive the treatment they need, without any stigma or any association with the penal system. Obviously the stage of development and the needs of children of any physical age vary widely, but there must be some dividing line. We believe that this line should be drawn at the statutory school-leaving age, and that no child under that age should be subjected to criminal proceedings. If society requires the child to remain at school, society may fairly be expected to ensure that he receives not only formal education but also training in social responsibility (Longford Study Group, 1964, p. 24).

We may note in this report, as in the Kilbrandon proposals, the aversion to criminal proceedings against school-age children and the references to the educational system as against the penal system to provide the necessary forms of social training. In point of fact these ideas were not really new in this country, having already been expressed in writing before, although they do not appear to have been taken

84

up on an official basis or by any political party in the past, so that their publication tended to attract interest on a limited scale in academic circles only.

It was toward the end of the second world war that a group of people who were members of the International Committee of the Howard League for Penal Reform met together to 'prepare a programme for reconstruction in the (penal policy) branch of government against the day when peace should come . . . of winning back for society the children and young men and women whom war had made rebels and outlaws', and they believed, 'that a wise policy in the treatment of young offenders should be the first charge of every Ministry of Justice in the New Europe.' (See Fry *et al.*, 1947, p. 5.) Contributors to the discussions included a number of well known criminologists and jurists who had fled to this country from Nazi oppression, as well as eminent men and women of public affairs in this country. They published the outcome of their discussions in book form and one of the contributors, Dr Max Grünhut, wrote a chapter entitled '*Competence and Constitution of the Juvenile Court*'. In this he suggested that the next step which should follow the establishment of a juvenile court system in any country should involve the transfer of such a system to an Administrative Youth Welfare Authority (sic) which would be a non-judicial body making use of educational and welfare services for dealing with young delinquents. He considered that any country in which such services were already well developed could afford to convert from the juvenile court system to this new type of agency, but retain a judicial system in the background to deal with disputed cases in which questions of personal liberty were in issue. He stressed that in this new system it would be essential to work in close collaboration with parents, for without their co-operation the system

85

could not function. Dr Grünhut took as his model the Scandinavian Child Welfare Boards in which all social welfare problems, including delinquency, which affect children come under one administrative authority irrespective of how the need for public intervention may arise.

There was therefore already a considerable body of knowledge and opinions in favour of a new philosophy for the treatment of juvenile offenders which the Longford study group could follow, and the ideas expressed by the group, although not exactly identical with either the Kilbrandon Committee's or Dr Grünhut's, had at least this much in common with them: avoidance of criminal proceedings for young offenders, and instead, merging the treatment of young offenders with that of other school-age children who require specialized provisions for any number of reasons. And this proved to be the line of thinking pursued in the Labour Government White Paper, *The Child, the Family, and the Young Offender*, which was published in August 1965.

The Government White Paper

Direct reference to the Longford report is made in the White Paper, and while the proposals are not the same, they are based substantially on the same philosophy. The Longford report envisaged the family service, backed by a family court to take care of disputed cases, to be the agency for handling delinquent children; the government for its part, wishes to introduce a special non-judicial agency for hearing and diagnosing cases which would be called 'the family council', working in concert with the family service which would provide the necessary treatment facilities. In essence the proposals include the following: in future children and young persons should be regarded

86

as falling into two categories: those under the age of sixteen and those between the ages of sixteen and twenty-one.
(We shall be concerning ourselves here with the first age
group only). By way of justifying the age limit set at sixteen, the White Paper states: 'Sixteen will soon be the
upper age for compulsory school attendance. It marks a
significant stage in the lives of many young people. It is
the age at which they begin to earn a living, at which many
may leave home, at which they may marry. The same
considerations lead to the conclusion that this should also
be the upper age for the special preventive measures which
are applied by law to those children who are in need of
care, protection or control and the age after which many
young persons should in general become subject to the sanc-
tions of the criminal law.' Next there are advanced four
specific reasons why juvenile courts are no longer thought
to be appropriate for dealing with this age group. These
are:

1. Children should be spared the stigma of criminality.
2. The main task of the courts appears to lie in deciding
    on appropriate treatment, since in the majority of
    cases facts in the offences that bring children before
    the court are not in dispute.
3. The present arrangements do not afford the best
    means of getting the parents to assume more personal
    responsibility for their children's behaviour.
4. Decisions about the type of treatment are made in
    the form of court orders, and these do not give
    sufficient flexibility in developing the child's treat-
    ment according to his response and changing needs.

All in all, the White Paper suggests that the juvenile courts
have outlived their usefulness and there is therefore no
mention of the compromise solution put forward by the

Ingleby Committee for the substitution of protective powers for criminal proceedings in the case of the younger age groups. The juvenile court system should be abolished and its place taken by a new body, the family council. Each local authority, county council and county borough, should set up such councils, the larger authorities more than one. These would act initially through the children's committees, but later, when the family service had been developed, through it. The family council's function would be to deal with all cases of delinquency and those requiring care, protection or control, and to work as far as possible in consultation with parents and with their agreement. The same agencies which now have powers to bring a child before a juvenile court, would retain the power to bring him before the family council. In the case of serious offences, or where the facts in allegations were in dispute, the matter would be referred to another agency to be established, the family court, which would be a special magistrates' court constituted to deal with such cases, and having also a wider jurisdiction, mainly in the province of civil proceedings affecting children and young persons.

So far as treatment is concerned, the family councils would have wide powers of prescription, essentially in conjunction and co-operation with the parents and with their agreement about the course of action to be taken. Treatment measures themselves would include provision for the payment of compensation by the child or his parents to anyone who had suffered loss as a result of the child's actions. It would also include supervision of the child by an officer of the children's department, or sending the child away for some form of residential training. The attendance centre would be retained which indicates that punishment as a form of treatment is not to be excluded altogether in the future. In the cases where the parent does not agree to the plan for treatment, the matter would be referred to the family court which would have powers to make compulsory treatment orders. The only form of compulsion which the family council could employ, if necessary in disregard of the parents' wishes, would be it could order a child for a limited period to an observation centre for assessment and recommendation as to the type of treatment likely to prove most beneficial in his case.

The approved school system as a separate entity would cease to exist, and the junior schools would be merged with the residential facilities of the local authorities.

As for staffing the family councils, it is envisaged that social workers of the children's service and other persons selected for their understanding and experience of children, would run them.

Mindful that the proposals would produce critical reaction from many quarters, and probably also anxious to iron out as many practical discrepancies as possible before drafting legislation, the government stated that they were published at that stage to stimulate discussion, adding that it was intended to consult organisations interested in these matters, and to seek the advice in particular of those who would have to operate any new system. The tenor of the paper makes clear the direction of the changes which are enshrined in the constitution of the family councils and treatment facilities. It remains to be seen however what their final form will be.

Reactions to the White Paper proposals

As might be expected, objections to the proposals were soon forthcoming. Naturally enough, magistrates and probation officers were among the most vociferous and

G

vehement of the various groups which expressed alarm about the propriety and possible consequences of removing delinquent children from the ambit of court proceedings. Their objections, like those of others not necessarily as directly connected with the juvenile courts, have been based, very largely, on ideological grounds, and since their views are sincerely maintained and reasonable, they cannot be dismissed simply as expressions of disappointment by two groups of people who are likely to lose some status by the abolition of a hitherto distinctive judicial system in which they had an important stake. Their objection rests largely on the grounds that under the new system, an executive body would be armed with powers which, by long tradition in this country, have belonged to the judiciary. More particularly, there is the point that a child may be deprived of his liberty when for instance, he is sent away for treatment to a residential establishment, and his parents may be deprived of his care, through executive action outside of the due process of law. This indeed is open to criticism. Even if one allows for the premise that this would be possible only if the parents agreed to such a course of action, it allows for little guarantee that some form of moral blackmail by a persuasive and sophisticated official agency might not overawe inarticulate parents, vulnerable to influence by officialdom, into agreement for the sake of forestalling further trouble with authorities. All this would take place behind closed doors, for there would be no press representative nor other independent observer present. In a court, on the other hand, the process of justice ensures that the rights of even the smallest subject are safeguarded, but there is no guarantee that this would be the case in the family council.

Another objection that has been voiced is that the shift from the concept of crime, punishment and responsibility,

90

which is endemic in the juvenile court system, to that of treatment based wholly on the needs of the offender, is to be deplored. Two adherents (Cavenagh and Sparks, 1965) of the juvenile court system writing shortly before the White Paper was published put it thus: 'In practice the concepts of criminal responsibility and punishment have an important function: for they *limit* what can be done *to* offenders in the interests of justice and individual liberty'.

There are answers to such criticisms. In the first there are already many situations where the executive has powers which affect the liberty of the individual and carries these out without abuse, and the provision in the new system for retaining the judicial system in the background is a vital safeguard. As to the second criticism voiced by Cavenagh and Sparks, it must be said that the whole purpose of the new procedure is to concentrate on treatment needs and therefore what is done for a child is done in the interests of his welfare.

What the White Paper proposals involve is a change in direction from the traditional, legalistic approach to a welfare approach, and this is exactly what the government proposes to bring about. One of its most influential spokesmen on juvenile delinquency, Lady Wootton, summed up the new philosophy when she wrote in the course of correspondence on the subject in *New Society* (29/7/1965): 'I submit that up to the compulsory school leaving age every child should be treated in an educational and not a penal atmosphere and should not be liable to any penal proceedings whatsoever.'

But in the end there is in fact no common point of agreement between two diametrically opposed viewpoints and one is left to choose between two philosophies.

Apart from ideological considerations, there are objections to the new proposals on practical grounds. In the main, they revolve around the present shortage of trained social workers, who would have the major responsibility for staffing the new service, and also on the general lack of availability of suitable treatment facilities. These shortages exist now and unless remedied, would hamper any system whatever its ideological basis.

Still further irritation has been caused by what one commentator (Morris, 1966) has suggested is the 'slack draftsmanship or the thinking that went into the White Paper; while the family council would appear to have the right of referring cases to the family court, the rights of parents and children for moving from the council to the court are far from clear'. There are other matters which are not made clear; here are two of them. First, while in the main the council can only act in agreement with the parents, it has overriding power to send a child away for a limited period to an observation centre. This could easily result in a disconcerting mixture of actions voluntarily agreed to by parents and compulsorily imposed ones, and as such could cause confusion to parents and children alike. Secondly, there is no mention of whether any legal representation for the parties before the council would be allowed. Presumably it was thought that this would bring in too much of a court atmosphere into proceedings which should be designed along social work rather than procedurally legal lines.

The proposed staffing of the family councils, by drawing on a mixture of social workers from the local authority children's departments and other persons selected for their understanding and experience of children, has also come in for criticism. It raises the question whether either professional or lay personnel by themselves can be trusted to come to right decisions; the former in case they overstep the mark of what the public might be prepared to accept, the latter because their lack of formal training in professional social work might incline them too often to fail to diagnose trouble and hence order the wrong sort of treatment.

These points however should not be allowed to overshadow the gains which could be made under the new system. The distinction between delinquent and non-delinquent children would disappear. The child would come to the notice of the family council because of his needs and not because he must stand trial for some anti-social act which someone is obliged to prove against him. The stigma of criminality would no longer attach to those children who at present still proceed to the juvenile court through the route marked 'delinquency'. The socially deviant child of school age would no longer be singled out for attention and treatment in a different way from the one who is now, for educational purposes deemed maladjusted and treated without recourse to a court. Other gains would follow as the preventive services became integrated with the new system, for earlier detection of children in need would be possible, and this could mean earlier treatment.

Conclusion

As was noted in the preface it is possible that the White Paper proposals, or at any rate something along those lines could become official policy in the foreseeable future after the results of the consultations with interested organisations have been evaluated by the government. The question that must be asked then is, will the inevitable changes in orientation bring about a reduction in juvenile delinquency? Certainly there will be changes in the tabulation of juvenile crime in the annual criminal statistics, but young boys, and to a lesser extent, young girls, will no doubt continue to go on shoplifting expeditions in multiple stores, break into warehouses, steal milk-money left on doorsteps or do any of the score of things that now merit the definition of crime. In the short term the projected approach to delinquency is unlikely to be more successful in reducing the extent of it than the current one has proved to do. All one can do is hope that the new approach coupled with preventive measures will in the long run, contain, if not actually reduce, the anti-social behaviour of children. It is likely to take a long time, and the beneficial effects of the new system may not be felt for a decade or more.

This book began with a statement to the effect that within little more than a century, social policy has been radically altered as the result of a profound change in attitude toward juvenile delinquency on the part of society. At one time the young offender was held morally as well as legally responsible for the crime he committed and in consequence, was expected to take his punishment however harsh it might be. In the course of time, ideas about moral culpability, legal responsibility and liability to punishment have undergone changes and these are reflected particularly in social policy. Some people would consider the changes to have been for the worse, as yet another manifestation of a nation that is failing in its inculcation of moral values and a sense of personal responsibility into the younger generation. Others, however, would view them as a natural and logical extension in the social development of a society which, while it feels concern to the point of taking certain actions, is certainly not frightened by the delinquencies committed by its younger members, and is therefore prepared to deal with them on essentially educational and social welfare, rather than predominantly legal, lines.

6
Suggestions for further reading

In order to discover more about the subject of social policy in relation to the young offender, the interested reader will be obliged to range widely over the field of published material. The references in the body of the text give some indication of the sources from which the material is drawn and provide signposts to the follow-up of the discussion. The object of this brief chapter is to furnish a further guide to some of the literature.

The subject matter of social policy has been treated by textbook writers mostly in relation to the social services and therefore only a few deal with the subject as it relates to young offenders. All the same, it will be of considerable value for the student to acquaint himself with some of the subject matter of social policy. For that reason he is recommended to read *An Introduction To The Study Of Social Administration*, edited by D. C. Marsh, (Routledge & Kegan Paul, 1965). It is written as a straightforward, largely descriptive account of social policy and its implementation through the social services. Another introductory and very informative book is *Social Policy* by T. H. Marshall, (Hutchinson, 1965). In this book Professor Marshall deals with the policy of governments with regard to actions which have a direct impact on the welfare of citizens, but apart from a brief passage on juvenile delinquency, does not touch upon the subject of crime. Nevertheless it still remains of interest to the student of delinquency who is new to the subject, as it indicates so well the formulation of thinking which goes into the devising and implementation of social policy. The first-mentioned book follows a similar pattern, except that it deals only with the British scene, and it does contain a Chapter in Part III by Richard Silburn, 'Offenders Against the Law'.

These two books form a useful background against which one may view the literature relating to the treatment, past and present, of young offenders. The historical development of this treatment, as indicated in official reports and legislation over the past 180 years, is covered in R. S. E. Hinde's *The British Penal System 1773-1950*, (Duckworth, 1951). The whole of this small but well-written volume is worth reading and Chapters VII and XI deal specifically with developments as they affected juveniles. It must be noted that since the book was published in 1951, the discussion does not extend beyond the Criminal Justice Act 1948. Chapter XIII of Part III in Max Grünhut's book *Penal Reform* (Oxford, Clarendon Press, 1948), deals with treatment reforms relating to juveniles in many parts of the world and stands as an authoritative account of the subject. As in the case of the book by Hinde, the work necessarily stops short of most recent developments. Another scholarly book, A. G. Rose *The Struggle for Penal Reform*, (Stevens and Sons, 1961) is essential reading. To quote from the foreword: 'Dr Rose traces the development of penal policy in England and Wales during the last 100 years, and the influence of voluntary societies upon that policy, in particular the Howard Association, the Penal Reform League and the Howard League for Penal Reform.' The book covers policy in relation to offenders of all ages and references to juveniles are distributed throughout the text but Chapters Eleven and Twelve are devoted to young offenders in particular. Jean Heywood's book, *Children in Care* (Routledge & Kegan Paul, 1965) is another work to be consulted since it includes valuable material relating to the changes in social policy toward delinquent and neglected children over the past 150 years.

A short but very useful discussion of the general principles of jurisdiction over juveniles can be found in the 'Report of the Committee on Children and Young Persons, (Ingleby Committee) 1960' Cmnd.1191, Chapter Three, paragraphs 52-113, which has a particular bearing on the currently debated question concerning the retention of the juvenile court system; a different viewpoint, on the same matter can be obtained by reading the 'Children and Young Persons (Scotland) (Kilbrandon Committee) Report 1964 (Cmnd.2306, Part I, paragraphs 5-81).

For a continuing account of policy, the Reports of the Home Office Children's Department should be consulted. The first of these was published in 1923. The most recent (1964) is that for the years 1961-1963 (H.C.155) and is obtainable from the Stationery Office. It may also be possible to obtain the Eighth Report published by H.M.S.O. in 1961. The reports have a separate section devoted to juvenile delinquency and the juvenile courts, and reproduce many of the more important memoranda and circulars issued by the government since publication of the previous report. Relevant extracts from the Criminal Statistics may also be found in them.

An acquaintance with criminology is essential to any understanding of the subject which has been discussed in this book. For a general, introductory English text, Howard Jones' *Crime and the Penal System* (University Tutorial Press, (second edition) 1962), is strongly recommended. The subject is discussed in non-technical language and a good deal of the material is concerned with the position of juveniles. A more advanced introductory work has recently been published; it is H. Mannheim's *Comparative Criminology* (Routledge & Kegan Paul, 1965) and comprises two volumes. To quote from the dust cover: it is 'the only full length modern textbook of pure criminology dealing with every branch of the subject in Britain.' It deals with the various criminological theories advanced in many countries in the course of more than a century and provides a very comprehensive coverage by one of this country's most distinguished criminologists.

For a description and discussion of juvenile court procedure, the student should read the book by J. A. F. Watson, *The Child and the Magistrate* (Jonathan Cape, 1965). It is easy to read and understand. The author writes with knowledge gained from his experience as Senior Chairman of the juvenile court for the Inner London area. The first edition came out in 1942 and since then the work has been continually revised and brought up to date. Another book, with an excellent fund of sources, on the general subject of penology, is N. Walker, *Crime and Punishment in Britain* (University of Edinburgh Press, 1965). Chapter X of Part III is devoted to young offenders.

The recent proposals for a change in direction of social policy relating to young delinquents, outlined in the government White Paper, *The Child, the Family and the Young Offender* 1965 (Cmnd.2742) (obtainable from H.M.S.O. 1s. 6d.) has given rise to a considerable number of articles, mostly in professional journals. Amongst these are: 'New Plans for the Young Offender' (*The Justice of the Peace and the Local Government Review'*, Vol. CXXXI No. 36), T. C. Morris, 'Struggle for the Juvenile Court' (*New Society* Vol. XII No.176), P. Boss, 'The Government White Paper Proposals Examined—Historical and Constitutional Background' (*Social Work Quarterly Review*, Vol. 24, No.2). A special number of the *British Journal of Criminology*, Vol. 6, No.2 contains contributions on various aspects on the topic by P. D. Scott, Lord Kilbrandon, W. E. Cavenagh, L. Neville Brown, F. V. Jarvis and B. J. Kahan.

The equivalent Scottish White Paper is entitled 'Social Work and the Community' Cmnd. 3065 issued by the Scottish Education Department, Scottish Home and Health Department. October 1966: The proposals in it have been clearly thought out. The document should be read.

Bibliography

BRAITHWAITE, R. M. (1951-52) 'Attendance Centres for Young Delinquents', *British Journal of Delinquency*, II, 245.

CARPENTER, M. (1851) *Reformatory Schools for the Children of the Perishing and Dangerous Classes and for Juvenile Offenders*, London: Bennett.

CAVENAGH, W. E. (1959) *The Child and the Court*, London: Gollancz.

CAVENAGH, W. E. and SPARKS, R. (1965) 'Out of Court?', *New Society*, Vol. VI, No. 146, p.9.

COHEN, E. W. (1949) *The English Social Services*, London: Allen and Unwin.

CURTIS COMMITTEE (1945-46) *Report of the Care of Children Committee* (Cmd. 6922), London: H.M.S.O.

DU CANE, SIR E. (1885) *The Punishment and Prevention of Crime*, London: Macmillan.

FRY, M. *et al.* (1947) *Lawless Youth*, London: Allen and Unwin.

GOVERNMENT WHITE PAPER (1965) *The Child, the Family, and the Young Offender* (Cmd. 2742).

GRUNHUT, M. (1948) *Penal Reform*, London: Oxford University Press.

GRUNHUT, M. (1956) *Juvenile Offenders Before the Court*, London: Oxford University Press.

HANSARD, H. C. (1847), XC, 430.

HANSARD, H. C. (1947-48), CDXLIV, 2138.

HANSARD, H. L. (1854), LXXXV, 579.

HANSARD, H. L. (1962a), CCXLIV, 815.

HANSARD, H. L. (1962b), CCXLV, 433.

HEYWOOD, J. (1959), *Children in Care*, London: Routledge and Kegan Paul.

HINDE, R. S. E. (1951) *The British Penal System 1773-1950*, London: Duckworth.

HOME OFFICE (1942) *Second Report on the Work of the Children's Branch*, London: H.M.S.O.

HOME OFFICE (1951) *Sixth Report on the Work of the Children's Department*, London: H.M.S.O. (May).

HOME OFFICE (1955) *Seventh Report on the Work of the Children's Department*, London: H.M.S.O. (November).

HOME OFFICE (1964) *Report on the Work of the Children's Department*, 1961-63, H. C. (March), 155.

HOME OFFICE (1965) *Juvenile Offenders and Those in Need of Care, Protection or Control (England and Wales)*, London: H.M.S.O.

INGLEBY COMMITTEE (1960) *Report of the Committee on Children and Young Persons* (Cmd. 1191), London: H.M.S.O.

JAMES, T. E. (1962) *Child Law*, London: Sweet and Maxwell.

JONES, A. E. (1945) *Juvenile Delinquency and the Law*, London: Pelican Books.

JONES, H. (1962) *Crime and the Penal System*, London: University Tutorial Press.

KAHAN, B. J. (1961) 'Approved School or Fit Person Order', *Child Care Quarterly*, Vol. XV, No. 2.

KAHN, A. J. (1963) *Planning Community Services for Children in Trouble*, Columbia University Press.

KILBRANDON COMMITTEE (1964) *Report on Children and Young Persons (Scotland)* (Cmd. 2306).

KING, J. (1964) *The Probation Service*, London: Butterworth.

LIVERPOOL, Chief Constable of (1962) *The Police and Children*, Liverpool: City Police Headquarters.

LONGFORD STUDY GROUP (1964) *Crime, A Challenge to us all*, London: The Labour Party.

MACK, J. A. (1962-63) 'Police Liaison Schemes', *British Journal of Delinquency*, III, 316-75.

MARSHALL, T. H. (1965) *Social Policy*, London: Hutchinson.

MAYS, J. B. (1965) 'The Liverpool Police Liaison Officer Scheme', *Sociological Review, Monograph No. 9*, pp. 185-200.

BIBLIOGRAPHY

MCCLINTOCK, F. H. (1961) *Attendance Centres*, London: Macmillan.

MOLONEY COMMITTEE (1927) *Report of the Committee on the Treatment of Young Offenders* (Cmd. 2831), London: H.M.S.O.

MORRIS, T. (1966) 'Struggle for the Juvenile Court', *New Society*, Vol. VII, No. 176, p.17.

PARKER, J. (1965) *Local Health and Welfare Services*, London: Allen and Unwin.

ROSE, A. G. (1961) *The Struggle for Penal Reform*, London: Stevens and Sons.

SCOTT, J. A. (1956) *Problem Families in London*, London County Council.

WILSON, H. (1962) *Delinquency and Child Neglect*, London: Allen and Unwin.

WALKER, N. (1965) *Crime and Punishment in Britain*, Edinburgh: University Press.

WATSON, J. (1965) *The Child and the Magistrate*, London: Jonathan Cape.